ELIZABETH REX

# Timothy Findley

with Paul Thompson

## *Elizabeth Rex*

HARPER
PERENNIAL

*For Martha Henry, Brent Carver,*
*Diane D'Aquila, and Peter Hutt*

*Elizabeth Rex*

Copyright © 2000 by Pebble Productions Inc.
All rights reserved. No part of this book may be
used or reproduced in any manner whatsoever
without prior written permission except in the
case of brief quotations embodied in reviews.
For information address:
HarperCollins Publishers Ltd.,
2 Bloor Street East, 20th Floor
Toronto, Ontario M4W 1A8

*www.harpercanada.com*

HarperCollins books may be purchased for
educational, business, or sales promotional use.
For information please write:
Special Markets Department
HarperCollins Canada
2 Bloor Street East, 20th Floor
Toronto, Ontario M4W 1A8

First published by Blizzard Publishing Inc. 2000
First HarperPerennial Canada edition 2003

National Library of Canada Cataloguing in
Publication

Findley, Timothy, 1930–2002
Elizabeth Rex / by Timothy Findley.

A play.
ISBN-13: 978-0-00-639253-8
ISBN-10: 0-00-639253-9

1. Elizabeth I, Queen of England, 1533–1603 –
Drama. 2. Shakespeare, William, 1564–1616 –
Drama. I. Title.

PS8511.I38E45 2003     C812'.54     C2002-904698-X
PR9199.3.F52E45 2003

RRD 9

Printed and bound in the United States
Set in Palatino

Come,
Let's have one other gaudy night: call to me
All my sad captains; fill our bowls once more:
Let's mock the midnight bell.

—*William Shakespeare*
ANTONY AND CLEOPATRA, *III, xiii*

*Elizabeth Rex* was first produced by the Stratford Festival and premièred at the Tom Patterson Theatre in Stratford, Ontario, on June 29, 2000, with the following cast:

| | |
|---:|:---|
| ELIZABETH | Diane D'Aquila |
| NED | Brent Carver |
| WILL | Peter Hutt |
| JACK | Scott Wentworth |
| CECIL | Bernard Hopkins |
| TARDY | Joyce Campion |
| PERCY | Keith Dinicol |
| HARRY | Paul Dunn |
| STANLEY | Florence MacGregor |
| HENSLOWE | Rita Howell |
| BEAR | Aaron Franks |
| LUDDY | Michael Fawkes |
| MATT | Evan Buliung |
| TOM | Damien Atkins |
| BEN | Andrew Burr |
| SERVANTS | Wayne Davis, Pragna Desai, Andy Pogson, and Rose Ryan |

Directed by Martha Henry
Sets and costumes by Allan Wilbee
Lighting designed by Louise Guinand

Original music by Stephen Woodjetts
Sound designed by Todd Charlton
Choreography and movement by John Broome
Fights directed by James Binkley
Assistant Director: Andrew Freund
Stage Manager: Lauren Snell
Assistant Stage Managers: Renate Hanson,
Milissa Rood, Helen Himsl and Michael Hart
Design Assistant: Bonnie Deakin
Lighting Design Assistant: Andrew McCaw

# Playwright's Note

I would first like to acknowledge the contribution of Paul Thompson to the development of this play. Paul not only directed the Stratford Festival's workshop of an early draft, but also—through all the subsequent drafts—directed private workshops in which the only participant was the playwright, who was asked to perform each of the major characters. It was in these "bear-pit" sessions that a better understanding emerged as to who these people were, and how they interacted.

This play was born in answer to a conundrum that has fascinated me for years: because women were not allowed to appear on stage in Elizabethan theatre, the female roles were played by so-called boy actors—but who played the women of a maturity and depth far beyond the range of any boy? Who played Cleopatra—Lady Macbeth—Mad Margaret? It seemed to me that there must have been actors in Shakespeare's time who had passed well beyond boyhood, and who therefore could undertake such strong and demanding female roles. Without such men, would Shakespeare have written such women? And so I invented a mature leading actor of female roles—Ned Lowenscroft.

Pondering the whole question of a contradiction of genders, I remembered that Elizabeth I often referred to herself as "a Prince of Europe" and even declared that in order to maintain her grasp on the British monarchy and to rule her England, she was called upon to be more man than woman.

Suddenly, a phrase drifted into my mind. *Elizabeth Rex*, "King Elizabeth."

Here, then, was the possibility of a glorious, theatrical confrontation—between the woman who throughout her reign had played the role of a man, and the man who in his theatrical career had played the role of a woman. To make the most of the confrontation, I decided it must take place at some moment when the monarch felt it necessary to recapture her womanhood, just as the actor finally required—for whatever reason—the full strength of his manhood.

History provided such a moment. Two years before her death, the Queen's lover, Robert Devereux, the Earl of Essex, raised a rebellion against her. If Elizabeth, the monarch, had to condemn him to death, where did this leave Elizabeth, the woman? Fiction was then able to step in and give the actor a disease that in those days was often fatal—syphilis. Was he man enough to face his own imminent death?

History offered further help. Essex, imprisoned in the Tower of London, was to be beheaded in the early morning hours of Ash Wednesday, 1601. On the eve of his execution, Shrove Tuesday, it is known that Elizabeth called Shakespeare and his actors—the Lord Chamberlain's Men—to perform in one of her palaces. She sought distraction from the torment of what her royal duty had forced her to do. It is not recorded which play was presented on that occasion, and so I was free to have it be *Much Ado About Nothing*. To me, Elizabeth would have loved the character of Beatrice, one of the strongest and most independent women in the Shakespeare canon. This way, I was also able to have the

Queen become intrigued by the actor who brought this woman to life.

History provided one more fascinating twist. The nobleman who was imprisoned with Essex for taking part in the rebellion was Harry Wriothesley, Earl of Southampton—the playwright's wealthy patron and, according to some, the true love of Shakespeare's life. (By the way, if Harry's name baffles you, it can be pronounced either of two ways: *Risely* or *Rosely*. We have chosen *Rosely* for the play.)

Shakespeare, who was actually writing *Hamlet* in this period, is shown to be in the early stages of creating *Antony and Cleopatra*—a play that was not performed until after the death of Elizabeth. Many scholars believe this was because it told a story too close for comfort to that of Elizabeth and Essex.

What emerged, for me, from this barn filled with contradictions and emotional conflicts, was a sense that neither gender nor sexuality, politics nor ambition, are as important as integrity. As Shrove Tuesday passes into Ash Wednesday, playwright, player, and Queen must come to terms with who they truly are, and how they will cope with the inevitable. This echoes Polonius's advice in *Hamlet*: "This above all, to thine own self be true." Or, as Glenn Gould was to declare to me a year before his death: "all that matters is that you become yourself."

*Timothy Findley*
STRATFORD, ONTARIO
June 2000

# Characters

The names in brackets are the characters played in *Much Ado About Nothing*, just before the main action of the play begins.


*The Lord Chamberlain's Men (in order of appearance):*
WILL: William Shakespeare, actor-playwright and share-holder of the Lord Chamberlain's Men; fifty-two.
NED: Edward Lowenscroft, actor; mid-thirties. (Beatrice)
JACK: Jonathan Edmund, actor; late thirties. (Benedick)
MATT: Matthew Welles, actor; twenties. (Claudio)
PERCY: Percy Gower, character actor; sixties. (Watch)
HARRY: Henry Pearle, actor; eighteen. (Hero)
TOM: Tom Travis, boy actor; late teens. (Margaret)
BEN: Benjamin Herlie, boy actor; late teens. (Boy)
TARDY: Kate Tardwell, the wardrobe mistress or " 'tire woman"; fifties.
LUDDY: Luddy Beddoes, character actor; fifties. (Friar Francis)
BEAR: Ned Lowenscroft's tame bear.

*The Court (in order of appearance):*
STANLEY: Lady Mary Stanley, early twenties; maid of honour to the Queen.
ELIZABETH: Queen Elizabeth I; sixty-seven.
HENSLOWE: Anne, Countess of Henslowe, lady-in-waiting to the Queen; seventies.

CECIL: Lord Robert Cecil, Private Secretary to the Queen; thirty-eight.

Servants, Watch, Boys, Men, etc.

# The Set

The play takes place in the whitewashed interior of a barn
in Stratford-upon-Avon on the night of April 22, 1616, until
the dawn of the following morning. At the rear, a barnyard
is visible beyond tall wooden doors that stand open. There
is an exit upstage right into the further reaches of the barn.
There are hay lofts above either side of the upstage area,
each reached by its own ladder. The upstage area is raised,
with two broad steps leading down. Slightly off centre, a
brazier waits to be lighted. A basket of fuel sits nearby.
Various theatrical accoutrements are also seen: some wicker
skips containing properties and costumes which spill over
their sides; a cluster of box-trees and a rosebush; a box of
books; a bundle of furled standards; a keg of ale on a tripod;
a barrel of water, plus a bucket; a prince's chair, a bench,
and some wooden stools. There is straw on parts of the
floor. Above the lofts, a banner is loosely hung, which
reads: "The Lord Chamberlain's Men." On the night of
Shakespeare's death, it is in this setting—filled with relics
of his London days—that the playwright conjures another
barn and another night—Shrove Tuesday, 1601.

# *Prologue*

---

(*The barn, Stratford-upon-Avon; night, April 22, 1616. The interior is lit with ghostly* L I G H T.)

N E D: (*Off, singing a cappella.*)
    Fear no more the heat o' the sun,
    Nor the furious winter's rages;
    Thou thy worldly task hast done,
    Home art gone and ta'en thy wages;
    Golden lads and girls all must,
    As chimney-sweepers, come to dust.

(*A bell tolls.*
*A* L I G H T *appears in the barnyard.*
W I L L *enters, carrying a lantern. He wears a long robe of the sort worn before retiring. Under this, he wears a loose shirt and hastily drawn on Jacobean trousers and hose. He is slippered. There is a scarf about his neck and woollen gloves on his hands. He is fifty-two years old.*)

W I L L: There you are, then—somebody's passing-bell . . .
    (*Lighting a taper from his lantern, he lights the brazier.*)
    Tomorrow, it will ring for me. "Young Will Shake-
    speare died this day . . ." That's what they'll tell you.
    "Died this day that was his birthday. Fifty-two years
    old . . . Lay back and died. In his bed. Like a child."

Trouble is—I'm not in my bed and I won't lie down. I'd
rather be out here, in my barn.

*(He looks about him, spies a box of books, and begins to rum-
mage as he speaks. He puts a small book, a notebook, and a
pencil in his pocket.)*

My whole life is out here—*(He flips the pages of a book.)*—
the whole of my life . . . I'd come here naked, as a boy—
straight from that river out there—throw my clothes on
the floor and climb into that loft and lie there dreaming
in the hay . . .

BOYS: *(Off, calling.)* Will! Will! Where are you? Hurry up . . .

*(SOUND: water, birds, insects.)*

WILL: All those summer days—scouring the banks of the
Avon for smooth, round stones—scaring up ducks and
foxes—kingfishers—swallows . . .

*(Distant dog barking.)*

. . . somebody's dog . . . Oh, God—I want it back.
Throwing stones that never reached the other shore.

*(He throws a book back into the box.
SOUND: a stone plunges into water.)*

And the games—the games—the games, and all my friends . . .

BOYS: (*Off.*) Will! Will! Over here! Over here!

WILL: . . . the river making off with our lives—all of us swept downstream and God knows where we'd land . . . Well—I landed here. Right where I began. This barn is the only theatre I have left. This—and the one in here. (*His mind.*) And these. (*The book box.*) Mere echoes of what there was. Cold now—for April. Not the Aprils I remember. So be it. That's what they'll say I died of—*a chill.* Went out a week ago—having spent the day, the evening, the night with my friend Ben Jonson. Two drunken playwrights—both of us overfed and over-aled. Stood in the rain, and the cold and the wind, and the wind blew all the way through me . . .

(SOUND: *a dog barks.*)

Who am I talking to? *Who goes there? Give me a moment! Let me have one—last—moment!!*

(*A ghost* BEAR *appears from the gutters and heads upstage centre towards the barnyard. As it passes* WILL, *he reaches one hand towards the figure, but the* BEAR *continues on and exits.*)

I know who you are! I know what's happening here! I know what's happening! Leave me alone! I could not—

I *cannot* write you! Oh—dearest Jesu—why in this final moment, *this?* This, that I could not and *cannot* achieve . . . the telling of that moment. The telling of that night.

(*He pulls a stone jar from his pocket and drinks. Then he goes to one of the skips and pulls out articles of costume.*)

What should a person wear to die in? I have been so many . . . lived so many other lives. And all the while, my own life burning down around me while I barely noticed it—failed to live it. And now, it's over. Nearly. Not quite. Almost. And that unwritten night . . . These were the flags they wore—the emblems of who they were: *the tunic of a soldier . . . the bodice of a queen . . . the bells of a clown . . . the gown of Beatrice . . .* purchased, I might add, at some expense—*and the cap of a scholar . . .*

(*Having laid the others aside, he regards the scholar's cap.*)

I put this on my head each time I wrote. It was my only ritual.

(*He puts it on as if it were the crown.*)

"Down it will come—and the words will follow. Flow." Or so I prayed.

(*He takes off the cap.*)

These are the only truths I know—I know no other

truths but these. We play so many roles before we die—
and then . . . we die.

(*The bell tolls nine.*)

I'm not ready. Not yet . . . Don't!

(*The dog barks.*)

Barking dogs . . . Shrove Tuesday. Ash Wednesday.
1601. The beginning of the ending of my world.

(*He puts on the scholar's cap, turns to the barn doors, and
quotes.*)

"You are welcome, masters. Welcome, all."

(*From the courtyard, four of the players drag on a cart with
props and a skip on board. The actors are costumed for* Much
Ado About Nothing. PERCY GOWER *jangles bells.* JACK
EDMUND *carries a tattered banner.* MATT WELLES *is the
drummer.* JACK *and* MATT *wear scarlet tunics. The fourth
player is a woman. They cross the stage. The woman moves to
the brazier. She pulls off her wig and throws it down.*)

NED: Shit!

(*Clearly, a man has spoken.
The* LIGHTS *alter. We are in the past.*)

# Act One

## SCENE ONE

(NED LOWENSCROFT *is in his thirties. Strands and tufts of hair hang down, and there are open sores on his head. He wears white make-up, with rouged cheeks and lips. His gown is black, the bodice already hanging open.*)

NED: Shit! Shit! Shit!

(*He tries to undo more of his costume.*)

WILL: You'll wear yourself out with shitting, if you're not careful.

NED: I'll shit when I please.

WILL: Mind what you do to that costume, Ned. It cost me a good deal of money.

NED: Piss on your money. If you spent more, you could afford a half-decent actor.

WILL: I assume you aren't referring to yourself.

NED: Damn right I'm not. I'm referring to that bitch, Edmund.

(*He removes a shoe and throws it at* JACK.)

WILL: Jack? Next to you and Dick Burbage, Ned, he's the
best we have.

NED: Best what? Arse-licker?

WILL: Now, now . . .

NED: Tell him to learn his lines!

WILL: Learn your lines, Master Edmund. (*To* NED.) Which
lines?

NED: Ask *him*. The bitch.

(*He throws a second shoe.*)

WILL: Why? How can Master Edmund name what he forgot?

JACK: (*Picking up the shoes.*) I forgot to say: "Tarry, sweet
Beatrice . . ."

NED: Yes! And a lot of good that does me now! Out there—
I near walked off the stage because you didn't call me
back.

JACK: It was only one line.

(*He throws the shoes at the skip.*)

WILL: Here! Mind those shoes!

NED: *Not* only one line! It was my cue to turn! I near fell off the edge. I near fell off the god-damned edge. I near fell off the god-damned rutting edge! The god-damned rutting edge, you god-damned rutting whore!

WILL: I think we get your point, Ned.

NED: No. You do not! (*He shouts in* JACK*'s face.*) Near fell off the god-damned rutting edge!! In front of the god-damned rutting Queen!! You god-damned rutting bitch!!

JACK: You've been drinking again, haven't you.

(NED *kisses him.* JACK *recoils in genuine horror.*)

Dear Christ in heaven! Don't! (*He wipes his mouth.*) Not on my lips, you bastard! Not on my lips, you diseased bastard . . . Oh, Christ . . .

(*He crosses to the bucket and throws water on his face.*)

WILL: The disease is not in his lips, Jack. His spittle will not harm you. "Tarry, sweet Beatrice . . ."

NED: Oh, God—what have I done . . .

WILL: Nothing. No harm. None. Say your next line.

NED: Oh . . .

WILL: Come along, now. "Tarry, sweet Beatrice . . ."

NED: "I am gone, though I am here; there is no love in you; nay—I pray you, let me go."

WILL: "Beatrice . . ."

NED: "In faith, I will go."

(NED *steps from the gown.*)

WILL: (*Whispering.*) Benedick . . .

JACK: "We'll be friends first . . ."

NED: "You dare easier be friends with me than fight with mine enemy."

JACK: "Is Claudio thine enemy?"

NED: "Is 'a not approved in the height a villain . . ." (*He now attempts to remove his underskirt.*) " . . . that hath slandered, scorned, dishonoured my kinswoman?" (*He tears the underskirt away.*) "O, that I were a man!"

(NED *wears tights, a shirt, and a bourrelet, which gives him the outlines of female hips.*)

JACK: There. Are you satisfied . . . my man?

NED: Maybe. Maybe not. I should not have kissed you.

JACK: True.

(WILL *picks up the discarded underskirt, sees it is ripped, and throws up his arms in despair.*)

NED: I should have "eaten your heart in the market place," you bugger! And me, near falling off the edge into the Queen's lap . . .

JACK: If you had, she would have loved you for it.

NED: I dare say. If I were not diseased . . . I should not have done that. Jack. I'm sorry.

JACK: It's gone, now. Washed away.

(NED *takes the underskirt from* WILL *and crosses to the skips, where he deposits skirt and bourrelet, removes a stone jar of liquor from its hiding place, and drinks.*)

PERCY: "I near fell off the edge. I near fell off the god-damned edge. I near fell off the god-damned rutting edge! The god-damned rutting edge, you god-damned rutting whore!" I wish I had that much to say.

WILL: Stop complaining—

PERCY: I have a right to complain. I'm old—and you never give me nothing to speak no more.

WILL: If you could keep a sentence straight, Percy, I might.

PERCY: Nothing to say. Not one word. Nor dancing. Nor the songs I once sang—in my youth . . .

MATT: We don't want to hear about your youth, old man.

PERCY: In my youth . . . *in my youth*, I played a prettier girl than any boy you ever saw. In my youth, I had a pair of legs that killed, in britches parts. Killed men dead! *Dead*—they did. I had a leg you'd hardly know was human. Men sent me flowers. Flowers in parcels. Parcels of them! Par-cels. In my youth . . .

WILL: In your youth I hope you had the sense to keep your mouth shut. You're tiresome as a wife.

PERCY: I put a lot of money in your pocket, Will Shakespeare. In my time—much money. You got no right to speak to me that way. I put a packet in your pocket. Me as Jacques. Me as Feste. Me as Shallow. "Jesu! Jesu! The mad days that I have spent . . ." You wrote that out for me, Will. And now, you give me nought to speak— *nought*—I that was your prince of clowns.

(*Three more players enter, carrying lanterns.* TOM *and* HARRY—*boys as women*—*and* BEN *as a boy.* BEN *carries a basket.*)

JACK: Any news? Surely we aren't stuck here for the night?

HARRY: Yes . . . All the others got away before the last bell. We're the only actors left.

BEN: There's a curfew. They've locked the gates!

HARRY: It's still not safe in the streets. Won't be, till the cannons fire in the morning. That's what they said.

MATT: Really?

(HARRY *nods.*)

Dammit—so we're still prisoners.

JACK: And—*voila!*—no London, no divine Olivia . . .

MATT: We'll never see *her* again.

JACK: Maybe you won't—but I will.

TOM: I'm not one bit sorry we're here. I've never been in a palace before.

BEN: I've never been out of London before. (*He hands the basket to* MATT.) Here's food we stole for them as didn't eat.

MATT: You're very good at that, young Ben. More than a useful talent for a starving actor.

BEN: We was fed in the kitchen! I had the whole of one chicken, all to myself. Tom wasn't hungry, was you, Tom.

TOM: No. They gave me wine and it made me sick.

PERCY: Tempting young boys. That's the way it was with me. Plies you with drink—then it's down with the britches and into the dark. You mind, Tom. I told you a thousand times.

HARRY: I was there. Nothing happened. I wouldn't let it.

PERCY: Men and women—each has dangers. You mark my words.

(TOM *removes his female clothing and throws it onto the floor. He still wears his female wig and make-up.* HARRY *removes only his wig.*)

NED: Oh, for God's sake! It didn't happen. Talk about something else!

PERCY: I could give you "all the world's a stage . . ."

ALL: (*Speaking in tired unison.*) " . . . and all the men and
women merely players . . ." (*Some make rude noises.*)

PERCY: It was only a suggestion.

MATT: Sit on it.

(PERCY *sits, and as he sits, he "farts."*)

PERCY: I can still play a fart on cue. I'm not a dead loss,
you know.

(*From the courtyard, there is distant laughter and applause.
Spirited* MUSIC *is heard—with pipes and drums.* TOM
*makes an attempt at a solo courtly dance.*)

BEN: Come along, Tom—this is the way they do it! You be
my lady and I'll be your lord . . .

(*They dance near* PERCY, *who joins in.* WILL *sits on the
steps, takes the small book from his pocket, and reads.*)

---

## SCENE TWO

TARDY: (*Off.*) Here! You lads!

(KATE TARDWELL, *known as* TARDY, *appears in the barnyard. She is slightly tiddly, and attempting to balance at least three hats on her head, while her arms are loaded down with skirts, jerkins, ruffs, sword belts, etc. She moves as if avoiding obstacles.*)

TARDY: Is nobody there? Help poor Tardy. It's me, fellows! Kate! Get busy, or I'll drop the whole lot in the yard manure—an' you'll wear 'em, stink or not! Seven hats, and four need mending—three white shifts, and two is torn. Them that ran to the city, 'fore the curfew was set. Look—they ripped half my stitches in their hurry. And none of you is better, stay or go!

(BEN, TOM, *and* HARRY *go to her and lift off parts of her bundles. The hats stay on her head; her spectacles sit on the uppermost hat, their arms around its crown.*)

Wantons! Stripping off these pretty pieces—throwing them in all directions! And only me to find them. Now, my spectacles is lost. Gone. And all this work to do before morning . . . You seen 'em? My specs?

(TOM *removes the spectacles from the hat and puts them on.*)

TOM: No, Tardy.

(HARRY *grabs the spectacles from* TOM *and puts them on.*)

TARDY: You?

HARRY: On your nose, last time I saw them.

(BEN *steals them from* HARRY *and puts them on.*)

TARDY: You?

BEN: Never.

TARDY: I know that voice. Don't give me *never*, Master
    Rascal! It's you took 'em off me twice before.

BEN: Never, Tardy. Swear.

(TOM *grabs the spectacles from* BEN *and puts them on*
TARDY*'s own cap, so they rest above her forehead.*)

TARDY: Well, one of you did. *Some*one did. I'll take my ale,
    now, thank you. If I can find my way.

(*She heads for the keg, bumping into* MATT *as she goes.*)

Who's that? You, is it, Master Matthew. Get me some
    ale, same as always—there's a good fellow.

MATT: Right away, Kate.

(*He goes to the keg and fills a tankard.*)

TARDY: (*Putting her hand out.*) There's fines for rending

'tires—and I want them now. Morning will come and London with it and I'll want more threads . . .

(*She goes about collecting pennies from the actors.*)

Pay up, clumsy louts and ruffians . . . Here! That was tuppence from you! None of that making off with my profits. I got expenses same as you and a husband's grave to tend, besides. Tore it straight through, you did, that doublet I mended only yesterday. (*She puts the collected money in a cloth purse.*) I never been in a Queen's barn before. It don't half smell horsy.

(M U S I C. *Cries of approval, applause—from off.*)

All them lords and ladies, dancing delighted, but the Queen does her dancing from a broken heart. Makes a person wonder what her Council's up to, don't it— what with Essex on the block. Proper bastard, that's what he is, that Essex. As for that other, the Earl of Southampton—the one she Towered with him—he's as much a proper bastard as his friend. The two of them— treasoners!

M A T T: (*Handing her ale.*) There you go.

T A R D Y: Bliss on earth . . .

J A C K: Don't tell me *you* were in love with Essex, too.

TARDY: I think not. He never pays his debts, either—same as you lot.

(JACK *and* MATT *laugh.*)

Oh, yes! A manly laugh. A woman gets used to man's laughter—the scorn of it—the leer of it. And the rage.

JACK: The rage, Kate?

TARDY: Aye. That a woman has more 'pacity for love than a man. So a fellow has to mock it—make it seem Cheapside, for fear we find him standing in the shallows when it comes to his own 'pacity for love.

MATT: 'Pacity, Kate?

TARDY: 'Pacity. Yes. Some such word. I heard it only once, but I know what it means.

NED: "She had a sweet capacity for love."

TARDY: That's it. A sweet capacity. *She* had, mark you.

NED: "And he had none."

TARDY: "And he had none." You spoke it, Master Ned. I don't remember where.

NED: *Love's Labour's Lost.*

TARDY: "A sweet capacity for love . . ." A well-writ
phrase.

WILL: We cut it.

(*She tries to set the empty tankard in place. It falls.*)

TARDY: See that? Without my specs, I'm blind as a belfry.
And my eyes required for six more hours of stitching. If
I discover one of you lads scuppered with them, there'll
be more than one beheading in the morning.

(*She starts off, up left.*)

JACK: You leaving us without the benefit of female company, Kate? We want your 'pacity . . .

TARDY: Hah! You'll never lack for female company, Master Edmund. Not till you hit the grave. And even there,
I'd have me doubts.

(TARDY *exits into the deeper reaches of the barn up left.*)

MATT: That's our Tardy—poor old woman.

NED: Best be careful. Next you know, she'll use your cod-
piece for a pin cushion.

(*He sits close to* WILL, *who is still reading the book.*)

WILL: Must you sit there?

NED: Yes. Do you always move your lips when you read?

WILL: Piss off.

NED: Are you trying to get away from us?

WILL: I'm already away from you.

NED: Escape? Is that why you read?

WILL: I read because I write. It is a necessity of the trade.

NED: Fascinating. And do you write because you read?

WILL: Stop that!

NED: I just wondered . . . (*He lays a finger on the open book and reads aloud.*) " . . . she received a whole succession of letters from him, begging her to visit him, but she treated him with such disdain . . ."

(WILL *snaps the book shut in exasperation.* NED *takes it from him and, finding the place, goes on reading.*)

" . . . she treated him with such disdain, that when she finally appeared it was as if she mocked him . . ." Are you still going on about this?

WILL: Yes. And will until I get it right.

NED: Liar. You could write it in your sleep. You're just afraid of it—thank God. (*Referring to the book.*) What is this?

WILL: Plutarch.

NED: (*Reading.*) " . . . and she came sailing up the river in a barge with a poop of beaten gold—its purple sails all billowed in the wind . . ."

(WILL *attempts to retrieve the book.* NED *evades him.*)

" . . . and while she languished, her oarsmen kissed the water with their oars of silver . . ."

MATT: She? What "she" is this? Sounds like Gloriana, going down the Thames to Essex House.

(MATT *removes his tunic and starts to wash off his make-up.*)

JACK: It's Cleopatra going down the Nile to Antony.

(WILL *lunges for the book and gets it.*)

WILL: Thank you.

(*He puts the book in his pocket.*)

MATT: What's the big secret? Come on—spill it!

JACK: (*Starting to wash away his make-up.*) The big secret is, our playwright has begun to fashion the tale of Antony and Cleopatra, but doesn't dare "finish" it. Too reminiscent of a recent love story . . . and too dangerous.

WILL: Leave it.

JACK: Too reminiscent of a certain passion . . . coming to a headless end tomorrow.

WILL: Leave it.

JACK: Too near the Queen's heart for the telling. And perhaps his own . . .

WILL: Leave it!

JACK: (*To* MATT.) It's me and Ned he wants to write it for. I wish he'd finish it.

NED: I won't be here to play it.

WILL: Don't say that, you cheap dramatic slut! Don't play your death! Live it! Damn you.

NED: So—are you going to save me? Doctor Shakespeare and his magic cure!

HARRY: Please, Ned. Don't.

NED: Don't yourself—my pretty rutting maid! Keep your bloody concerns to yourself.

HARRY: I only . . .

NED: It's my death, Harry. Mine! Leave me to it. *All* of you!

LUDDY: (*Off—roaring.*)
But when I come to man's estate,
With heigh-ho, the wind and the rain,
'Gainst knaves and thieves men shut their gate,
For the rain it raineth every day.

---

## SCENE THREE

(LUDDY BEDDOES, *one of the company's character men, is manhandled into the barn by two young Men.* LUDDY *is costumed for the role of Friar Francis in* Much Ado. *He continues to sing while the others talk.*)

FIRST MAN: There you go, then. And stay there.

SECOND MAN: (*To all.*) Mind you *all* stay. There's a curfew and the Watch has dogs. If you value your heels, you won't go running.

FIRST MAN: Pah! Actors! Drunken louts, the lot o'them . . .

(*The two Men exit.*)

MATT: So you got left behind like us, did you?

LUDDY: It's getting cold out there.

MATT: I thought you'd be on your way to Cheapside by
now.

LUDDY: Somebody put up the fire.

NED: Put it up your . . . self.

LUDDY: Can't. Me hands is too cold.

(HARRY *takes fuel from the basket and feeds the brazier.*
LUDDY *moves down to take advantage of its warmth.*)

WILL: I see. They caught you seducing another battalion of
women—is that it?

LUDDY: Well, I just been taking advantage of my apparel,
that's all. Oh—these country kitchen-girls! I told this
lass—"There's such a thing as Friar's Rights, you
know." I said: "You never heard tell of Friar's Rights?
Why," I said, "the Bishop shall hear of this, and he'll set
you a penance!" "Oh," she says, quaking, "oh," she
says. "I never knew. Don't tell." "Well," I said, "well,

seeing as how you repent," I said, "you might do your penance here and now. After all," I said, "isn't it Shrove Tuesday—a day set down for penance?" And she said, "What penance might that be, sir?" And I said, "Penance comes by numbers, child . . ." (*He cups imaginary breasts.*) " . . . two of these, and one of these." (*He gropes himself.*) And then I said, "There's a room 'neath the stair, just there—a closet full of linen for the table. Pure white linen—a suitable bed for a penance." And off she came with me, just like a lamb! A perfect triumph. "Friar's Rights!" Oooh! I pray you, Master Will, that I should play the Friar more often. Small parts have large rewards.

WILL: I don't want to know about your *rutting* parts.

LUDDY: Oh, now, Master Will . . .

NED: I was taken once, beneath a stair.

LUDDY: And was there linen?

NED: No. It was done standing up. By the man who had me first . . .

LUDDY: What—your father?

(NED *strikes him.* LUDDY *lunges, but others restrain him.*)

Here, now!

NED: You . . . You filthy . . . You god-damned filthy old man. I hope to Christ she poxed you.

LUDDY: It's you that's poxed, my lad! It's you that's patched with the pox! You that's got running sores of the pox! Not me! Not me! I wouldn't touch a boy—nor a *man*—not if you put me on the rack! You, with it up your arse! Or your own up someone else's! If you'd put it where it belongs, it wouldn't have killed you!

(*The* BEAR *calls, off.*)

JACK: Be quiet, Luddy.

LUDDY: Calling me a filthy old man—and him a whore!

JACK: Be quiet.

LUDDY: A person ought not appear on a public stage with the likes of you, Ned Lowenscroft.

NED: Then why don't you quit, you fiddling old fart.

(*The* BEAR *calls, off.*
*He begins to exit upstage.*)

I'm going to feed the bear.

(NED *exits.*)

HARRY: (*To* LUDDY, *on the verge of tears.*) You bastard.

LUDDY: That's right—defend him. Kiss his bleeding arse.

HARRY: But—he's dying, for Christ's sake! *Shut up!*

JACK: Come on, you two. Calm down. Luddy, drink some ale.

LUDDY: I only meant to tell a good story . . . I thought *Friar's Rights* was funny as hell. But I'm not a filthy old man.

PERCY: Of course not. You're not even sixty yet!

WILL: (*To* HARRY.) You all right?

HARRY: Yes. I guess. He says that bear's the only friend he has.

WILL: Well, we know that isn't true. Don't we.

HARRY: He won't let me touch him, Will. "Pox," he says. "The pox." Pushes you away, as if he didn't want a friend.

WILL: He played a Beatrice this afternoon, the likes of which we may never see again.

HARRY: Ned can play anything—

WILL: Except his own life, damn him.

HARRY: He saved that bear! No one else would have done that. Only Ned. I *saw* him. Got right down and saved it from the pit—the dogs. Near dead, it was.

WILL: I believe you, but—

HARRY: But if a bear can be saved—why not Ned?

(*There is distant* MUSIC *for a formal dance.*)

PERCY: I was a dancer once. All the courtly dances . . . Come along, Ben, you'll have to do this one day—and do it right!

(PERCY *plays the lady, teaching* BEN *the dance.*)

Ta dum . . . ta dum . . . ta *dum!*

(WILL *sits in the prince's chair, takes out his pencil and notebook, and starts to write.*)

---

## SCENE FOUR

(LADY MARY STANLEY *appears in the barnyard, cloaked and hooded. She carries a lantern. The dancing continues until* LUDDY *sees her.*)

LUDDY: 'Ere, 'ere. Who might this be?

STANLEY: Gentlemen . . .

MATT: Madam?

STANLEY: Are you what remains of the Lord Chamberlain's Men?

MATT: We are. The others escaped . . .

(WILL *kisses the notebook and pockets it.*)

STANLEY: So, you have been told about the curfew.

LUDDY: Aye . . . for fear the people will rise in Essex's
behalf.

MATT: What might we do for you, madam?

STANLEY: Have you a chair?

MATT: A chair? (*To* LUDDY.) Have we a chair?

LUDDY: (*To* PERCY.) Have we a chair?

PERCY: (*Hurrying down to* WILL.) Have we a chair?

(WILL *rises, revealing the prince's chair.*)

WILL: A chair.

PERCY: (*Decisively.*) Yes. (*He hurries back to* LUDDY.) We have a chair.

LUDDY: (*To* MATT.) We have a chair.

MATT: (*To* STANLEY.) Yes, madam. We have a chair.

STANLEY: What sort of chair?

MATT: (*To* LUDDY.) What sort of chair?

LUDDY: (*To* PERCY.) What sort of chair?

PERCY: (*Hurrying to* WILL.) What sort of chair?

WILL: This sort of chair. Take it and show her.

(PERCY *turns and calls back to* LUDDY.)

PERCY: Take it and show her . . .

TOM and BEN: (*Together.*) Take it and show her!

WILL: (*Pulling at* PERCY'*s arm.*) *You* take it and show her.

PERCY: Yes. Yes. Of course. Me. I'll take it . . .

(*He picks up the chair and starts upstage with it.*)

I haven't had this much business to do in a dog's years!

(*He carries the chair up to* STANLEY *and sets it down with a flourish.*)

Madam—the chair.

OTHERS: The chair!

STANLEY: (*To* MATT.) Have you a cushion?

MATT: (*To* LUDDY.) Have we a cushion?

LUDDY: (*To* PERCY.) Have we a cushion?

PERCY: (*Blankly.*) Have we a cushion . . .

(*He turns, but* WILL *cuts him off.*)

WILL: Yes.

PERCY: We do?

WILL: There's a bum-roll up Harry's skirts. That should be cushion enough for anyone.

HARRY: My bum-roll?

WILL: Yes. Take it off.

(WILL *lifts* HARRY's *skirts, revealing his bourrelet.*)

HARRY: (*Untying the bow.*) I only kept it on to keep me warm . . . It's mine and I want it back.

(WILL *carries it to* STANLEY.)

WILL: There. It is the curse of men's bodies, madam, not to have hips. For the playing of women, this is worn.

STANLEY: (*To* HARRY.) Was it you who played the Lady Hero this afternoon?

WILL: Yes. That's Harry Pearle.

STANLEY: You were charming, Master Pearle. And I thank you for your . . . your hips.

HARRY: You're welcome.

STANLEY: Yes. This will do nicely. Thank you. (*To* MATT.) Have it put in the chair, and the chair down by the brazier.

(MATT *does so.*)

WILL: Why, madam?

STANLEY: Because, sir, we are coming in.

(*She exits into the courtyard.*)

MATT: Does anyone know who she is?

WILL: Presumably, one of the Court ladies.

MATT: A truant lady, in that case. Shouldn't she be with
the Queen?

LUDDY: Who cares where she ought to be. She's coming in
here!

(*He finds a mirror and begins to correct his appearance.*)

PERCY: I doubt she'll be interested in the likes of you.

LUDDY: More likely me than you, old man. Jesu! Make
way for the life of an actor! We are notorious! Even the
Court ladies seek us out. Who would stay with the
dowdy old Queen, knowing *we're* out here in the barn!
Not me, I wouldn't.

(STANLEY *returns, preceded by two hooded women.*)

Dowdy old Queen and her crazy vigil. Downright
bloodthirsty, that's what it is. Imagine! To cut off your
lover's head! Lover—ex-lover—whatever. *Reprobate*
lover! That's it! He tried to bring her down from the
throne and . . .

(*The women enter and make their way to the chair.*)

Here, here! (*To* JACK.) Three of 'em!

(*He steps forward.*)

STANLEY: Thank you. No. (*Pause.*) Madam.

(*She indicates the chair to one of the hooded women. The woman sits, pulling aside the skirts of her cloak. A foot is offered, wearing a boot, which* STANLEY *removes and sets aside. The second foot is offered, and its boot removed.* STANLEY *replaces the boots with brocade slippers. The woman draws back her hood. All the men except* WILL *fall to their knees.* WILL *bows his head.*)

ELIZABETH: What hour is it?

STANLEY: Not yet ten, Madam.

ELIZABETH: Up—up. Enough amazement. Give me some drink. I am dry.

JACK: There is nothing but ale, Your Majesty.

ELIZABETH: Then ale is what I want. *Now.*

(HARRY *draws a tankard of ale from the keg.* ELIZABETH *stares at* JACK. JACK *stares back.*)

ELIZABETH: (*To* JACK.) And you, sir? You are . . . ?

JACK: You saw me this afternoon, Majesty. I was Benedick.

ELIZABETH: You stare as though you had never seen a
    woman you could not have.

HARRY: (*Handing her the tankard.*) Madam.

ELIZABETH: And you?

HARRY: I was Hero, Madam.

ELIZABETH: Your health, Master . . . ?

HARRY: Pearle. Henry Pearle, Your Majesty.

   (*He curtsies.*)

ELIZABETH: You curtsy by instinct, Master Pearle?

HARRY: No, Madam. By habit. It is the gown that curtsies.

ELIZABETH: Very nicely said. And who else is here? Have
    we Master Shakespeare?

WILL: Yes, Majesty.

ELIZABETH: I enjoyed your play. To the extreme.

WILL: Madam.

ELIZABETH: I especially liked the character of Beatrice. I have much sympathy with her.

WILL: Madam.

ELIZABETH: There was a song I liked. "Sigh no more." It suited my mood. And Beatrice had a line . . .

(STANLEY *whispers to her.*)

"I will live a bachelor." That suited me, too. I must tell you, Master Shakespeare, I liked her better before she was joined to the Benedick.

WILL: Yes. And was easier to write . . .

ELIZABETH: More wit, than once she was joined with him. Yes?

WILL: Yes. Indeed.

ELIZABETH: When my sex is joined with yours, whatever else we lose, we also lose our wit.

(*She loosens her cloak, revealing a white dress and ropes of pearls.*)

I have come here to be in your company, Master

Shakespeare. I require distraction. And I warn you—I shall keep as many of you as I can on your feet till dawn.

WILL: Madam.

(*The third woman, the elderly* COUNTESS OF HENSLOWE, *lowers her hood.*)

ELIZABETH: Will none of you gentlemen help these ladies from their boots?

(MATT *steps forward and as he kneels before* STANLEY, *it is clear that she is attracted to him. Looking up, he catches her staring—and reciprocates. She hands him slippers, drawn from a pocket inside her cloak.* BEN *removes* HENSLOWE's *boots—while she, being old, supports her- self on a cane.*)

I love a barn. I've always felt safe in a barn. Because of the animals, no doubt. All the animals in a barn are benign—excepting the bull and the boar. (*She looks pointedly at* LUDDY.) One must be wary of them. But— I love the smell of horses, cattle—hay. Such a warm safe place. I trust that you are comfortable.

WILL: Yes. Yes. Absolutely.

JACK: Just like home.

ELIZABETH: And you lads there—well played—and pretty faces.

PERCY: I was a boy once, too. One of the Children's Players of the Chapel Royal.

ELIZABETH: And played the boy's part?

PERCY: No, Madam. I played the lass. Men sent me flowers . . . *parcels* of them . . .

JACK: Not again, Percy. Not again.

ELIZABETH: I dare say I might have seen you, Master Gower.

PERCY: She knows my name!

ELIZABETH: But of course I do. Percy Gower was a clown of great repute, many years gone. I remember you for your exquisite falling down.

(*She begins to wander the stage, lifting up properties and bits of costume, exploring them at random.*)

PERCY: *Exquisite.* Oh, Madam. *My exquisite falling down!* You hear that? Of course, it's true I fell down with much style. A proper tumbling fall, I had. And was famous for it. Also, for my dancing.

ELIZABETH: I do not recall your dancing.

PERCY: Oh, but that was in my *lady-days*—in skirts.

(ELIZABETH *holds* NED*'s discarded gown against her,
and gives its skirts a kick.*)

ELIZABETH: In my *lady-days*, I was a dancer, too, Master
Gower. I was a dancer, too. Tra-la!

(*She tries to dance.*)

I've spilt my ale on this pretty gown.

WILL: No harm done, Madam.

(*He turns away, furious—the cost!*
ELIZABETH *holds out her tankard at arm's length.*
STANLEY *takes it and passes it to* HARRY.)

STANLEY: More.

HARRY: (*Tankard to* LUDDY.) More.

LUDDY: (*Heading for the keg.*) More . . .

PERCY: (*Snatching the tankard.*) Mine! (*Embarrassed.*) My
turn . . .

(*He draws ale and carries it to* ELIZABETH.)

ELIZABETH: This gown was on your Beatrice, this afternoon, Master Shakespeare. When she mourned the death of Hero.

WILL: Yes.

ELIZABETH: And worn with grace. I wish I were an actor.

WILL: There are those who claim you are, Madam.

ELIZABETH: What? A *man?*

WILL: No, Your Grace. But one who performs with great skill.

(PERCY *arrives with the ale, which she exchanges for the gown.*)

ELIZABETH: "I cannot be a man with wishing, therefore . . ." What is the rest of that?

WILL: "I cannot be a man with wishing, therefore, I will die a woman with grieving."

ELIZABETH: "I cannot be a man with wishing—therefore I will die a woman." (*She toasts* WILL.)

WILL: " . . . with grieving."

ELIZABETH: I did not mean to say *with grieving!* I will not grieve! No grieving. None.

(HENSLOWE *wavers.*)

Someone bring the Countess a stool, a chair, a bench . . .
whatever. She is old.

(TOM *brings a folding chair.* HENSLOWE *sits.*)

Dearest Anne, it is not I who makes the night. Forgive.

HENSLOWE: Madam, there is no need.

ELIZABETH: You have stayed beside me all my life. If any
of you gentlemen require a lesson in loyalty, look to
Anne, Countess of Henslowe. By example, she is all
you need to know.

(*The bell tolls.* ALL *listen.*)

Ten o'clock. Nine hours remaining . . . in this watch.

(*The distant* MUSIC *begins an excessively sedate dance
tune.*)

I want brighter music than that. One of you go and say so.

(LUDDY *starts away.*)

Not you, Friar. They would not believe a friar had come
from me. No. Master Edmund—you shall go. They will
believe the Queen has sent them Benedick.

(JACK *grabs his scarlet tunic and puts it on as he starts away.*)

You have not yet received my permission, sir.

JACK: Madam?

ELIZABETH: Your back, sir, has *impudence* written on it.

JACK: My apologies.

ELIZABETH: I trust it is not written on your face. *Look at me, sir!!*

(JACK *turns.* ELIZABETH *is shaken by his resemblance to Essex.*)

Are those your true colours?

JACK: No, Madam. But they'll be useful in the Court.

ELIZABETH: Your eyes—what colour are they?

JACK: Blue.

ELIZABETH: Blue. Yes. Blue. They would be, wouldn't they.

JACK: Your Grace?

ELIZABETH: All Irishmen have blue eyes. And . . . You
    may go.

(*He does not.*)

    You may—*go*—sir.

JACK: Madam.

(*He exits through courtyard.*
TARDY *enters from up left with an armful of damaged costumes, still wearing her spectacles on her cap. She dumps the
costumes upstage.*)

TARDY: If you lads is interested, there's a gutter back there
    for the horses. Makes a good latrine for a man standing.
    Not for ladies. I said to this large white mare, I said: "If I
    beg your pardon, missus, do you mind if I use your
    straw for lady-matters?" And she says: "Neigh!" (*She
    laughs and begins to exit up left.*) "Neigh," she said! You
    can have that one, Master Will, if it pleases you . . .

(*She exits.*
ELIZABETH *laughs.*
*The dogs bark.*
*The Watch escorts* JACK *back to the doors.*)

JACK: Madam—the dogs . . .

ELIZABETH: (*Turning.*) Are you the watch?

WATCH: Madam.

ELIZABETH: He takes a message from the Queen. Let him
    pass.

WATCH: Your Majesty.

(*The Watch and* JACK *exit.*
*TARDY re-enters from up left, now carrying a sewing bas-*
*ket and a hat. She is oblivious of the new arrivals.*)

TARDY: What is it you lads do to these poor hats?
    Squished all down round the crown—their innards
    gutted. Worse than if a fowler had been at them! And
    still my specs lost.

(TARDY *comes to* ELIZABETH, *who cautions the others*
*to silence.* TARDY *stares at the Queen's gown and fingers*
*its sleeves—peering at them closely.*)

Here! Who said you could wear that? That's my best
    Lady Capulet, I warrant. You aren't to traipse around
    in that! So. Which one are you? Got up like that, I
    wouldn't know you.

(*She touches* ELIZABETH*'s face.*)

You Master Ned, playing your games on Tardy again?
    He's always doing that. Dressing up for the wrong
    play. Master Saucy!

ELIZABETH: What is your name, madam?

TARDY: Here. Whose voice is that?

ELIZABETH: It is me, madam. *I.*

TARDY: Mercy—you don't half do it well . . . The hair's a
  wonder. And them pearls . . .

  (ELIZABETH *smiles and lowers the spectacles onto*
  TARDY's *nose.* TARDY *steps back.*)

  Lord love us! You mean I put my hands on the Queen?

ELIZABETH: Indeed.

TARDY: Oh—that I should ever wash them off. These
  hands were on the Queen's own person. You ought not
  to have let me, Madam.

ELIZABETH: Tell me your name.

TARDY: Kate, Your Majesty. Kate Tardwell.

ELIZABETH: Are you really blind as you seem?

TARDY: Lord, Madam—I'm blind *because* I seam! These
  that I have are *seamstress-eyes.*

  (ELIZABETH *laughs.*)

Got over many years of tiny stitching. I can still find my way with a needle, mind you. It's the world at large that confounds me.

ELIZABETH: It confounds us all.

TARDY: (*Indicating* WILL.) Not him, it don't. He sorts the world the same way I sort my threads—unravels it— and sews it back together. Same as he sews his people.

(*She takes a stool and sits near the lantern light, setting her basket beside her.*)

ELIZABETH: There's a commendation for you, Master Shakespeare. A tailor of lives, is that it?

WILL: Perhaps. But it takes an actor to wear them.

(ELIZABETH *holds up a scarlet tunic, taken from the pile of clothes that need mending.*)

ELIZABETH: Benedick wears one like this. And Claudio.

WILL: Captains' tunics. Yes.

ELIZABETH: Worn for the wars, is that it? Scarlet to bleed in, Master Shakespeare? How blunt of you. How unsubtle. Your Benedick—your Claudio—they almost seem to be platonic lovers. I distinctly caught an echo of my lords now resting in the Tower. Was this intentional?

WILL: Not intentional. Circumstantial. All soldiers tend to love their comrades.

ELIZABETH: Not to say *worship*. You, that were Claudio— bring your tunic here.

(MATT *does so*. STANLEY *watches him*.)

TARDY: There's one of them tore already. Don't you go spoiling the other.

ELIZABETH: (*To* MATT.) Hold it up.

(*Each holds up a scarlet tunic*.)

There. You see? The very shape and colour of two headless men. No love between them, now—no bonding of allegiance—riding into the streets—raising their swords—*against their Queen*.

(ELIZABETH *snatches* MATT*'s tunic away from him*.)

TARDY: Here! Mind them!

ELIZABETH: (*To* WILL.) I think this one belongs to you. Take it as a memento of Southampton—he that was your patron.

WILL: Madam . . .

ELIZABETH: Were you invited to speak?

(ELIZABETH *puts her hands into her tunic's arms.*)

I wore such a man . . . once.

(*She extracts her arms.*
*Beyond the courtyard, the dogs bark.*)

---

## SCENE FIVE

ELIZABETH: (*To* LUDDY.) Friar?

LUDDY: Oh. That's me. Yes.

ELIZABETH: Why did you call my Lord Essex a reprobate?

LUDDY: Did I?

ELIZABETH: "Her lover—ex-lover. Her reprobate lover
. . ." You were not reciting lines. I know a rehearsal of
lines when I hear one. They speak by rote in Council
every day. *Her reprobate lover!!* I think you do not know
the meaning of the word.

LUDDY: Oh—oh—Madam . . .

ELIZABETH: I also think I saw you play the part of Falstaff, once. The word describes him perfectly. Debauched! Crapulous! Licentious! Dissolute! Swinish! Hoggish! *Bestial!* Would the Queen invest her love in such a man? Would she?

LUDDY: Madam—Majesty—Your Grace—I meant no more than . . .

ELIZABETH: No more than what?

LUDDY: Than to express the . . . the people's view . . . their horror at his sedition . . .

ELIZABETH: The people love him! Worship him! Have you never heard him praised? For his courage—for his stature—for his beauty?

LUDDY: No. No, Madam. No. He was . . . he was . . . he *is* a traitor!

ELIZABETH: Not *reprobate*. Learn your language. The word you seek is *ingrate*. *Ingrate!* A word with which every man is imbued—and every woman, familiar. Go.

LUDDY: Madam?

ELIZABETH: Go! You look like my father risen from the grave . . . And you argue like a weathercock. You shall not gain my favour. Take yourself to bed . . . (*She sees* PERCY.) . . . and Master Gower, too.

LUDDY: Take him to his . . . bed?

ELIZABETH: Now.

LUDDY: Treating us like children.

WILL: Yes—and why not?

ELIZABETH: Yes—and why not. (*To* TARDY.) And those lads, too—they should be abed.

TARDY: Madam . . .

(TARDY *gathers* BEN *and* TOM. *Meanwhile,* LUDDY *prods* PERCY.)

PERCY: Who's that?

LUDDY: Me. And keep your hands to yourself.

PERCY: I was having such a naughty dream.

LUDDY: Yes—well. You can keep your naughty dreams to yourself.

PERCY: "Jesu! Jesu! The nights that I have spent!"

(PERCY *and* LUDDY, *using the ladder, exit into the loft, where we see them settle into the hay.* TOM *and* BEN *begin to exit with* TARDY.)

ELIZABETH: (*To* BEN.) And where will you sleep in this barn?

TARDY: There's a hay rick yonder, Your Majesty. I'll see them safely to bed.

ELIZABETH: Go with your 'tire mistress, then. Go on.

(*The three of them exit up left.*
ELIZABETH *moves to where* HENSLOWE *is sleeping.*)

See how life bends us, Master Shakespeare. To live. To be—until we become entirely who we are—a bent old woman sleeping in a chair . . .

(*She kisses the top of* HENSLOWE's *head.*)

HENSLOWE: (*Waking.*) Oh . . . Majesty . . . I was dreaming.

ELIZABETH: Sweet dreams, I trust.

HENSLOWE: No, Madam. Horses.

ELIZABETH: (*To* WILL.) Her husband died beneath a horse. It fell. In the hunt . . .

HENSLOWE: Down it went—and him beneath it. In my dreams, he is always there. In my dreams, I am always young. In my dreams, I have not aged a single year since he died. How can one so young be so old? Every morning, the mirror lies . . .

(*The distant* MUSIC *begins again—with a lighter touch.*)

ELIZABETH: Good. That's better music. Perhaps now that damned Irishman will return.

(ELIZABETH *holds out her tankard to* STANLEY, *who goes for ale. Meanwhile,* NED *enters up left, leading the* BEAR *by a chain.* ELIZABETH *does not see them.*)

STANLEY: Madam . . .

ELIZABETH: (*Listening to the* MUSIC.) Be still.

STANLEY: But, Your Grace . . .

ELIZABETH: I have asked for *silence!!*

NED: (*A bit tipsy.*) Who the rutting hell is that?

ELIZABETH: *Silence!*

NED: (*To the* BEAR.) Luddy's brought in the fishmonger's daughter . . .

STANLEY: *Sir!!* How dare you!

NED: Oh, dear—a pair of 'em! Two bawds, *braying*.

(*He "brays," and then sings.*)

> Two bawds went a-braying, O!
> Two bawds went a-braying!
> Two braying bawds for laying! O!
> Two bawds went—

WILL: Ned. Tarry, sweet Beatrice.

(NED *turns, sees* ELIZABETH, *and falls down.*)

NED: Dear Jesus Christ! Oh, dear Jesus Christ!

ELIZABETH: Why is the Lady Beatrice lying on her face?

(*The* BEAR *stands up and ambles down towards* NED.)

STANLEY: Oh—oh—Madam.

ELIZABETH: Has someone brought me a bear? Did I ask for a bear?

STANLEY: No, Madam.

ELIZABETH: Is he dangerous?

WILL: Not at all. He's quite well tamed.

ELIZABETH: Is he yours?

WILL: He belongs to Master Lowenscroft.

ELIZABETH: Beatrice has a bear! Wonderful! May one approach him?

WILL: Yes.

HARRY: Ned sleeps with him.

ELIZABETH: In a bed?

HARRY: Oh, yes. In the bear's arms. Here, they've been sleeping behind the bars in the granary—so's the bear won't frighten the horses—nor the dogs get near the bear.

ELIZABETH: Good bear. Sweet bear.

(The BEAR stands and "speaks." ELIZABETH caresses his head.)

Master Lowenscroft, get up. I want an introduction to your bear. Has he a name?

NED: Harry.

ELIZABETH: I can't hear you.

WILL: Harry, Madam. He said *Harry*.

ELIZABETH: Shush. I want to hear it from him. From Beatrice.

WILL: Get up, Ned.

NED: Can't.

ELIZABETH: Rise!

(NED *rises*.)

And the dear bear's name?

NED: Harry. (*Mischief occurs to him. He smiles.*) Harry Wriothesley.

ELIZABETH: (*To* WILL.) *Your* Harry, then. Southampton that is in the Tower with Essex.

NED: Some would have him brought from the Tower.

ELIZABETH: And some would not. He plotted against me.

NED: Not against the Queen. Only for Lord Essex.

WILL: Ned...

ELIZABETH: And what has Southampton's name to do with bears?

NED: The bear was baited, Madam. Almost to death, by dogs. Everyone crying for his blood. I bought him from the keeper. Bears should go free.

ELIZABETH: You think Southampton is bear-like, Master Lowenscroft? Or merely baited.

NED: Baited.

ELIZABETH: By me? Or by circumstance...

NED: Circumstance didn't put him in the Tower.

ELIZABETH: The Law Towered him. The Law... his peers.

NED: And if his peers had set him free, what would you have done then? Concur? Or sent them all to the Tower for their lack of judgment.

ELIZABETH: You have a great deal to say, for a woman.

NED: Yes. But I can shed *my* woman. (*He removes his cloak, revealing tights and a long white shirt.*) Here today—and gone tomorrow.

ELIZABETH: Your impertinence may be charming, Master Lowenscroft. It may also destroy you.

NED: I'm already destroyed.

ELIZABETH: Oh?

NED: The pox. As you can see . . .

ELIZABETH: We are all poxed, Master Lowenscroft—one way or another. Life is a pox. It leaves its scars on all of us.

NED: This pox kills, Madam.

ELIZABETH: Life kills. That is its purpose. Have you ever played the part of a queen, Master Lowenscroft?

NED: In *The Tragedy of King Richard the Third*, I played King Henry's widow.

ELIZABETH: Margaret, then.

NED: Yes.

"Can curses pierce the clouds and enter heaven?
Why, then—give way dull clouds to my quick curses!
Long die thy happy days before thy death;
And after many lengthened hours of grief,
Die neither mother, wife, nor England's queen!"

(*Absolute silence.*)

Unquote. (*He curtsies and rises.*) I also play Titania—
*Queen of the Fairies!*

(*He "swishes" past* ELIZABETH *and drinks from his jar.*)

ELIZABETH: You have an extraordinary candour, Master
Lowenscroft. Had you forgot I am your sovereign?

NED: No, Madam. I had forgot I was myself.

ELIZABETH: I admire your honesty. And, this night, I
invite you to play whatever you choose. Whatever
role—whatever temper. Will that fellow never come
back?

WILL: Which fellow is that, Madam?

ELIZABETH: Your Benedick. I forget his name.

WILL: Edmund. Jonathan Edmund.

NED: Oh, he'll never come back. Not our Jack. He's in there
bouncing all the ladies of the Court.

ELIZABETH: Bouncing?

NED: Yes, Madam. Bouncing—trouncing—*pouncing!* With
a hey, nonny-no—our Jack has gone a-bouncing-oh!

STANLEY: Master Lowenscroft . . . The Queen!

NED: The Queen? Has the Queen never bounced? *Bouncing—trouncing, and off with his head!* I thought that's what this was all about.

WILL: Ned.

ELIZABETH: Leave him. He proves an excellent sparring partner—not unlike your other fools.

NED: "Look then to be well edified when the fool delivers the madman."

(WILL *moves towards* NED.)

ELIZABETH: No, I say. Leave him. Let him be.

(*Commotion in the courtyard. Voices—dogs.*)

---

## SCENE SIX

(WILL, MATT, *and* STANLEY *move to protect* ELIZABETH. HENSLOWE, *who has nodded off, wakes and stands with some effort.*)

CECIL: (*Off.*) Call off your dogs, sir! Call off your dogs!

(CECIL *enters. Seeing* ELIZABETH, *he sweeps the floor with his hat.*)

Your Majesty.

(*The dogs fall silent.*)

ELIZABETH: Have you come to give the actors lessons in excess, my lord? You were told I should not be disturbed.

CECIL: Your Grace—I have been commissioned . . . (*Seeing the others.*) Perhaps I should introduce myself . . .

ELIZABETH: I know who you are, Pygmy. What is this *commission?*

CECIL: Madam, as Private Secretary to Her Majesty, I cannot speak freely before strangers. (*To the others.*) Go.

ELIZABETH: Stay.

CECIL: But, Madam . . .

ELIZABETH: They will stay, Pygmy. Come to your commission.

(*With elaborate gestures,* CECIL *begins to loosen his cloak.*)

Without all that flamboyance. Just tell me.

CECIL: A petition has been delivered.

ELIZABETH: In whose behalf? (*To* MATT.) Bring me some ale. (*To* CECIL.) In whose behalf?

CECIL: In behalf of the Earl of Southampton, Madam.

ELIZABETH: Oh. (*She looks at* WILL.) You should be interested in this. (*To* CECIL.) From whom?

CECIL: His countess, Your Grace.

ELIZABETH: Eliza Vernon—damn her. Read it.

CECIL: (*As he seeks more light.*) Oh, Madam! God in heaven! There's a bear!

ELIZABETH: Yes. That's Harry Wriothesley. Why not read your petition to him? It comes from his wife.

CECIL: His *wife?*

ELIZABETH: (*To the* BEAR.) Your Grace, I give you Lord Robert Cecil. Pygmy—Harry. (*To* CECIL.) Get on with it.

CECIL: I...I...I...I...I...

ELIZABETH: *Read!*

CECIL: I . . . Oh, Madam . . . This communiqué was put into my hand for delivery to Your Majesty.

(*No response.*)

Very well . . .

(*He breaks the seal.*)

(*Reading.*) "Gracious Sovereign: In addressing Your Majesty on the occasion of my husband's imprisonment, I beg Your Majesty to recall that time when she looked upon my heart as bonded to her own—those happy days when I was Your Majesty's companion . . ."

Three "Majesties," Madam!! In a single sentence, Madam! Surely this is excess. I should be very wary, Madam, if I were addressed in such an obsequious manner. *Very* wary, Madam! Three "Majesties"—in the salutation alone!

ELIZABETH: Your definition of *excess*, Pygmy, surprises me, when you gave four "Madams" to three "Majesties."

CECIL: Madam?

NED: Five.

ELIZABETH: Proceed.

CECIL: Uhm . . . Yes . . . Madam . . .

NED: (*Sotto.*) Six.

CECIL: (*Reading.*) " . . . I mourn the passing of that happy
time with all my heart—as one would mourn the death
of happiness itself . . ." Oh, Madam. The poor dear child.

ELIZABETH: The "poor dear child" is a common whore.
My father would have adored Eliza Vernon. He had a
taste for whores. But these were and are my Glories.
(*She crosses to Stanley.*) Eliza Vernon was chosen for her
virtue, her grace, her beauty—intelligence—modesty
. . . (*At* MATT.) *And her virginity.* This poor child is now
the wanton countess (*At* WILL.) of *your* damned
Harry! Yes? He ran from your embrace to hers—from
your love to hers! Yes—and at your bloody urging!
Pregnant! Pregnant! Under my protection—in my
dominion—pregnant!

WILL: He married her.

ELIZABETH: Hah! Married! My father married my
mother! And after they were married he Towered her! I
did the same . . . I did the same to my once beloved
Eliza—and her husband. Towered. Imprisoned for a
pregnancy. They were children. Children! She was . . .
seventeen. Seventeen. I . . . Oh . . .

CECIL: Madam . . .

(*The dogs bark.*)

ELIZABETH: Damn him. Damn Southampton! Not a
month ago—not three weeks ago, he joined with Essex
in their rebellious return from Ireland to steal my
crown—my England. Not to say my life!

WILL: No, Madam . . . *No.*

ELIZABETH: You vagabond from reality! There were
swords in the streets! I pray to God you never get hold
of my life and place it at the mercy of your pen! You are
incapable of facts. There were swords in the streets—
two of them raised by Essex and Southampton. Spare
me your histories—your histories are full of lies. (*To*
STANLEY.) Mary? Finish this appeal.

(STANLEY *takes the letter nervously and reads.*)

STANLEY: "In memory of those times, I beg Your Majesty
to restore your former love of me. Grant my husband
pardon for his deeds. His apparent treachery—his
insubordinance were *deviations* only, born of his exces-
sive love of order, and his fear that Your Majesty was
being led astray . . . by . . ." (*Unwilling to say "Lord
Robert Cecil."*) " . . . others of your Court, whose per-
sonal ambitions placed Your Majesty's integrity in
jeopardy."

(CECIL *turns away.* WILL *watches him.*)

ELIZABETH: Finish.

(*Seeing* STANLEY*'s distress,* WILL *takes the letter and reads.*)

WILL: "In raising his sword against your Royal person, my husband meant only to bring Your Majesty's attention to this matter. What seemed to be sedition was nothing less than loyalty."

ELIZABETH: *Seemed? Seemed!* (*She snatches the letter.*) That sword Southampton raised was not a *seeming* sword. Nor was it a *seeming* alliance he formed with Essex! Seemed! Seemed! I will give you *seemed.* Pygmy! Take this page and burn it!

(CECIL *takes the letter with a smile, crosses to a lantern, and inserts the letter until it catches fire, throwing the residue into the bucket.*)

CECIL: Done.

ELIZABETH: In your play this afternoon, Master Shakespeare, there was a line I shall never forget—a sentiment crystallized in two short words. I know you will know which words I mean. Say them—and bring this moment to a close.

WILL: No, Madam. I—

NED: "Kill Claudio."

ELIZABETH: Thank you.

---

## SCENE SEVEN

ELIZABETH: (*To* WILL.) You are too forgiving. You
spared him. Claudio. For all his villainy—for all his
willingness to believe the worst of that poor girl, you
spared him. (*To* MATT.) You—you played that devil—
am I right? Claudio?

MATT: I did.

ELIZABETH: You should be drawn and quartered.

MATT: It was only a play, Madam.

ELIZABETH: Oh, yes. Yes. *Only a play*. Just as Southampton would have us believe. He merely *played* the villain.
(*To* WILL.) Were you lovers?

WILL: Madam?

ELIZABETH: Lovers. You and Harry Wriothesley. I have
been given (*She glances at* CECIL.) copies . . . anonymous . . . of certain poems . . .

WILL: Poems?

ELIZABETH: Beautiful, passionate, tender poems—all addressed to a tender, passionate, beautiful young man . . .

WILL: There have been many such poems written over time. The Italians excel at them.

ELIZABETH:
"Shall I compare thee to a summer's day?
Thou art more lovely and more temperate . . ."

CECIL: Doesn't sound like Italian to me.

ELIZABETH: They're credited to you, Master Shakespeare. These poems have your voice. A most distinctive voice. Unique. Were they addressed to him? Southampton? Most poets would be glad to claim them. But then—they were written to a traitor, weren't they?

WILL: Not that I'm aware of. No.

ELIZABETH: I wonder if any such poems have been written for my Lord Essex. Perhaps in Southampton's hand.

WILL: Your Majesty mistakes the nature of their relationship.

ELIZABETH: What? No love poems? Surely you can't believe that. Why, I was told that when Southampton left the Tower—three years ago—on the first occasion of his being imprisoned there, he leapt upon his horse and rode straight off to Essex, leaving his countess in the dust *and* his newborn child! Straight off to Essex!

WILL: Madam . . .

ELIZABETH: The sheets must have been so hot, I doubt Essex House stood in need of fires for weeks!

WILL: Madam—

ELIZABETH: (*Shouting.*) Months!! Damn them!! Damn you!! Damn all men—every last one of you!!

NED: Stop shouting!!

(ELIZABETH *looks at him—amazed. He smiles.*)

You'll frighten the bear.

CECIL: Madam—I am being discourteous here. The Countess Southampton will need some reply. And . . .

(*The bell starts to strike eleven.*)

ELIZABETH: Tell her I said *no.*

CECIL: Indeed—though I must remind Your Grace that— some days ago—Your Grace gave promise of an audience to the Countess.

ELIZABETH: The promise is broken.

CECIL: But—

ELIZABETH: The promise is broken!

CECIL: (*Deep bow.*) Madam . . .

(*He exits through the courtyard. The dogs bark.* CECIL *shouts at them. Silence.*
NED, *still slightly drunk, has gone to the keg.* HARRY *joins him when he sees* NED *can't locate a tankard.* ELIZABETH *listens to the bell while watching* HARRY *and* NED.)

HARRY: Here, let me.

NED: No. No, damn it. Leave off. Oh, Jesus Christ in heaven! Look at this. I'm bleeding. Blood—running sores. Putrid. And everything itches—everything itches! I will go mad. Oh, God . . . What am I going to do? What am I going to do?!

HARRY: Be quiet. Sit down.

(*He cleans* NED's *hand with a wet rag.*)

ELIZABETH: (*To* WILL.) So, another hour. (*Pause.*) Is this a love story?

WILL: Yes.

ELIZABETH: Will he die? The Beatrice?

WILL: Yes.

ELIZABETH: Have there been physicians?

WILL: (*Regretting the cost.*) Oh, yes. Every medicine and every torture they can devise. They've burned him with turpentine—purged him with cypress and anointed him with mercury. Nothing changes. No matter how much money, nothing works.

(JACK *appears in the doorway. The* BEAR *moves over to* ELIZABETH. *She pets it gently.*)

ELIZABETH: How did it happen? Does he know who it was?

WILL: A soldier—so he tells it.

ELIZABETH: One of mine?

WILL: Are there others?

ELIZABETH: Of high or low rank?

WILL: He's dead. And best left in peace.

ELIZABETH: Dead of the pox?

JACK: No. Dead of Ireland.

WILL: He died in one of those chance encounters with an
Irish bog. We are told he strayed in a moment of panic,
after the enemy had pulled him from his horse—and
perished. By sinking. He drowned.

ELIZABETH: In Ireland . . .

JACK: Yes. In Ireland.

(*The dogs bark viciously.*
*The* BEAR *stands up and cries out.* HARRY *crosses and*
*leads him away.*)

HARRY: (*Turning.*) It's the dogs, Madam. They remind him
of the pit. He forgets he's free.

(HARRY *and the* BEAR *exit.*)

---

## SCENE EIGHT

(*In the courtyard, there are voices. The dogs quieten.* MUSIC
*is heard—a dance tune full of spirit and gaiety. Two male*

*Servants of the royal household enter, carrying a camp table with three small gilt chairs piled on top of it. Two female Servants follow, carrying wicker baskets.* STANLEY *speaks to a male Servant, who exits and shortly reappears with three military camp chairs. Meanwhile,* STANLEY *supervises the unpacking of dishes, goblets, cutlery, food, and wine. A cloth is spread, the table set, candles lit.* ELIZABETH *concentrates on* JACK.)

ELIZABETH: You were such a long time absent, Master Edmund . . . I trust you were properly entertained.

JACK: I hope this music is more to Your Majesty's liking. I spoke to the musicians, as you charged me.

ELIZABETH: And did you dance, sir?

JACK: Yes.

ELIZABETH: What was her name?

JACK: I danced solo, Madam. I gave them some of my jigs.

ELIZABETH: I see. And nothing else?

JACK: And nothing else.

ELIZABETH: Then what is this?

(*She draws a white lace handkerchief from his tunic.*)

JACK: I found it.

ELIZABETH: In whose hand?

JACK: In no one's hand, Madam. I found it on the floor.

ELIZABETH: (*Handing him the handkerchief.*) You play the man too well. You even dare lie to the Queen. You may escort me to the table.

(*They move towards the table.* NED *hovers.*)

(*To* NED.) Are you hungry?

NED: No. Thirsty.

ELIZABETH: There is wine here, sir.

(*She sits and gestures for* NED *to do likewise.* NED *sits and pours wine.*)

And where in Ireland are you from, Master Edmund?

(*She gestures "sit!"*
JACK *pulls out a chair, but remains standing.*)

JACK: Dublin, Your Majesty.

ELIZABETH: Dublin. I had thought it a city more enamoured of the Church—of God and of bookish inclination. Is it not the site of your only university?

JACK: Yes, Madam.

ELIZABETH: And yet you rose from it with a sword in your hand.

JACK: I have no sword, Madam.

ELIZABETH: Ah, yes. I still mistake you . . .

JACK: It may be you do not, Your Grace.

ELIZABETH: Oh?

JACK: Whatever else I am—I am still an Irish man. And I will not sit with you.

(*He pushes the chair back in place and moves away. Pause.*)

ELIZABETH: Master Lowenscroft? Tell me—would you truly be a woman?

NED: Never.

ELIZABETH: Why? Why would you not be a woman— when you play her with such skill?

NED: I would rather be housed as I am.

ELIZABETH: Housed?

NED: In this . . . male flesh.

ELIZABETH: It gives you so much pleasure to be a man?

NED: Did I say it was a pleasure?

ELIZABETH: No. But there was pleasure in your voice.

NED: Then my voice betrays me.

ELIZABETH: If your voice betrays you, it is your voice that tells the truth.

NED: As your voice does, whenever you speak his name.

(ELIZABETH *throws her wine in his face.*)

Ess-ex!! You love him . . .

ELIZABETH: I love no one.

NED: Liar.

ELIZABETH: What?

NED: Liar!!

ELIZABETH: (*Enraged.*) You poxed buffoon!!

NED: (*Taunting.*) You overpainted effigy!!

ELIZABETH: (*Screaming.*) I'll have you drawn and
quartered!!

NED: (*Roaring.*) You should be stewed in brine!! And
pickled!! Kept in jars!!

ELIZABETH: (*Hissing.*) You poisonous—

NED: Poisoned!!

ELIZABETH: —toad!!

NED: Ha!!

ELIZABETH: Hagh!!

NED: Hagh!!

ELIZABETH: You Beatrice in britches!!

NED: And you . . . King Hen-er-y in skirts!!

(*A distant bell is heard—but not chimes. They all listen—
sobered.*)

ELIZABETH: The final call for penance . . . If tomorrow is

to come, we must all be forgiven. And here we are without a priest.

WILL: Might that forgiveness include the Earls of Essex and Southampton?

ELIZABETH: No. God may forgive them their sins, but I will not forgive their treachery.

WILL: But Madam, if God can be merciful, why not the Queen?

ELIZABETH: I cannot be merciful!! It would be the death of England!!

WILL: And if England should die?

ELIZABETH: I might as well not have lived.

WILL: And have you?

ELIZABETH: I killed the woman in my heart, that England might survive . . .

WILL: And so—you have already played the murderer . . .

ELIZABETH: You! You that fabricated every king of England—and their queens. God knows what you will write of me! I will be a monster under your hand. And I am not a monster.

WILL: Then, what are you? Is it not true you will kill your lover in the morning? And is that not monstrous? You tell me you have killed the woman in your heart . . . and now you want to kill the man who gave that woman life. Why?

ELIZABETH: Because I love him. And if, because I love him I spare him, I will then have killed the man in me who is England's only defence against her enemies. I will not spare him. Nothing will shake me in this. Nothing. Oh, God. Oh, God . . . if only I had your capacity for womanhood, Master Lowenscroft. Then at least I could mourn him.

(NED *turns away to find his jar—he stays in the shadows and drinks.*)

Say it. Tell me what you are thinking, actor.

NED: I am thinking that I am in the Tower with Essex—and that both of us wish there was a safe, dark place where we could hide from death.

ELIZABETH: Your problem is that you have forgotten you're a man. Listen to me. *Listen.* I will strike a bargain with you. If you will teach me how to be a woman . . . I will teach you how to be a man.

NED: It's too late . . .

*(The bell rings. Midnight.*
*The* LIGHTS *dim, except on* WILL, ELIZABETH, *and*
NED.*)*

ELIZABETH: No. It is not too late. We are moving from the
day of penance into the day of ashes. *(She crosses to the
brazier.)* Come here. Kneel down. There.

*(She reaches all the way into the brazier.)*

WILL: Madam!

ELIZABETH: Be still. *(She dips her fingers into the ashes.)* Be
still.

*(*NED *kneels beside her. She marks his forehead with ash.)*

   *Qui tollas peccata mundi, miserere nobis; qui tollas peccata*
   *mundi, suscipe deprecationem nostrum.* Almighty and
   everlasting God, who hatest nothing that thou hast
   made . . . create and make in us new and worthy hearts
   . . . *(She smudges her own forehead with ash.)* Will no one
   say amen?

*(*WILL *looks at them. Slowly, he removes the scholar's cap,*
*goes to the doors, turns for one last look—and exits.*
MUSIC.
*The last we see is* ELIZABETH *and* NED *in a decreasing*
*ghostly light. End of Act One.)*

# Act Two

## SCENE ONE

(ELIZABETH *is seated on a pillow on the floor, writing on
a lap desk.* NED *sits huddled by the brazier.* HENSLOWE
*dozes alone.* JACK, MATT, *and* TARDY *have found other
places to rest. The table and gilt chairs have been moved to
one side. The four Servants are seated around the stage. Cold
moonlight can be seen.*
WILL *enters from the courtyard and stands for a moment in
the open doorway. He carries the scholar's cap and his notebook.*)

WILL: Well—I have seen to my necessities. And more. I
have restored the contents of my jar. I would gladly
take my jar to the grave, but a man can't bend his elbow
in a wooden box.

(*The bell chimes four times.*)

Four o'clock. Ash Wednesday. And here they are
where I left them—all their endings still unwritten. (*He
puts on the scholar's cap and refers to the notebook.*) "If you
will teach me how to be a woman—I will teach you
how to be a man . . ." And if that man—that woman—
could be found, lives might still be saved . . .

(ELIZABETH *signals to a Servant, who steps forward. She hands over a folded paper. As the Servant exits, another Servant takes away the lap desk.*)

And what was on that page—a life? Or a death? If that letter does not provide a pardon, in just three hours we will hear a cannon fire in that yard out there—the signal that Essex is dead—the last of a relay of cannon fire that will play through London until it crosses the river to us. What then will be the subject of her grief? His death, or her own weakness that she cannot kill without remorse? Let us see which one of these will be the first to break the silence.

(*He puts on his cap and begins to write in his notebook.*)

ELIZABETH: (*To* WILL.) What are you writing there?

WILL: I'd rather not discuss it, Your Grace.

ELIZABETH: But I demand it. I've never seen a writer writing before. How fascinating. Is it your Cleopatra play?

(*He closes his notebook.*)

WILL: (*Lying.*) Yes, Madam.

ELIZABETH: Are you ashamed of it?

WILL: No.

ELIZABETH: Why, then, must you make a secret of it? Is it scandalous?

WILL: It has its moments.

ELIZABETH: Let me see. (*She takes the book and reads.*) "You play the man too well. You even dare lie to the Queen." But these are my words. Mine. What is this?

WILL: Madam, I am a writer. It is what I do.

ELIZABETH: And I am your subject—is that it?

WILL: No, Majesty. I am your subject.

ELIZABETH: Very clever—though there's nothing new in that. But why am I in this book? Why am I in here? Speak.

WILL: I am attempting to create a monarch, Madam. A monarch's words are of interest to me.

ELIZABETH: (*Regarding a page.*) "Noblest of men, woulds't die? Hast thou no care of me? Shall I abide in this dull world . . . ?" Who is this?

WILL: Cleopatra. When Antony is dying.

ELIZABETH: (*Reading.*) "Hast thou no care of me . . . ?"

NED: (*Reciting, overlapping.*) "Hast thou no care of me?
Shall I abide in this dull world, which in thy absence is
no better than a sty?"

ELIZABETH: You have this by rote.

NED: Some of it, Majesty. I was to play it, had I lived.

ELIZABETH: (*To* WILL.) Am I your Cleopatra? (*Pause.*) Is
your Antony, then, my Essex?

WILL: It had occurred to me.

ELIZABETH: Damn you!

(*She throws the notebook at him.*
ELIZABETH *drifts up to the skips and fingers the black
gown worn by* NED *earlier.*)

_____

**SCENE TWO**

(TARDY, *at the table, takes a bit of food.*)

ELIZABETH: Mistress Tardwell.

TARDY: (*Her mouth full.*) Madam?

ELIZABETH: A word with you about this stitching . . .

(*She holds out the black dress.* TARDY *crosses to her.*)

You mentioned a large white mare . . .

TARDY: (*Not understanding her drift.*) Oh yes, Madam. Very large and very white. Queen of the horses—and a wonder. Like yourself.

ELIZABETH: I believe you said you had spoken to her . . .

TARDY: I did?

ELIZABETH: Yes. About *lady-matters.* (*She does a subtle "dance."*)

TARDY: Oh! Yes. *Lady-matters.* Well! What a density I am. She'd be delighted, I'm sure. Seeing as how she accepted the likes of me, another queen would be more than welcome to share her straw.

ELIZABETH: Thank you.

TARDY: (*Leading* ELIZABETH *up left.*) Mind you, we mustn't wake them boys. They have all-seeing eyes in the dark . . .

(*As they exit,* ELIZABETH *sets the gown down. Seconds later,* STANLEY *enters from the courtyard, does not see* ELIZABETH *and rushes off, up left.* STANLEY *returns and picks up the black gown, retreating with it into the barn up left.*)

ELIZABETH: (*Off.*) Where have you been? I want that Beatrice gown—now!!

---

## SCENE THREE

NED: (*Indicating the notebook.*) What's in there? More of Antony and Cleopatra dying? Nothing you write is complete without a death—is that it? Show it to me.

WILL: It's only notes. But look, if you must.

(NED *takes the book and flips through the pages.*)

NED: Darkness. It's all about death and darkness. And this! (*He reads.*) "Ah, women, women, look—our lamp is spent. It's out . . ." (*Looking around.*) Like hell it is! We have a dozen lamps and I'll light every one. (*He calls out.*) Harry! Every rutting lantern shall be lit!! (*He runs to the up left exit.*) Harry! Harry! Lights! (*He places the notebook in his tights.*)

(HARRY *enters. He now wears only tights and a shirt.*)

HARRY: Are we on fire?

NED: Not yet. Get busy. I want every lantern lit.

HARRY: Every?

NED: Yes! In all the world! Make light. There——those. That one and that one. And that one there.

(HARRY *begins to light various other lanterns.* PERCY *and* LUDDY *climb down and do the same.*)

LUDDY: What's this? Has everyone gone mad?

NED: Yes! Yes! Mad!!

(*He sings with manic energy.*)

But let them go,
And be you blithe and bonny,

ALL: (*Joining in, singing.*)

Converting all your sounds of woe
Into hey nonny, nonny!

NED: (*To* WILL.) There aren't any songs in here. There's no one singing.

WILL: There will be . . . there will be . . .

NED: What?

WILL: Music. Dancing. Feasting . . .

NED: Ah! Now—there we have what's missing here.
*Feasting.*

WILL: It's Lent, for God's sake.

NED: Not in Egypt!!

(ALL *cheer.*)

Harry? Luddy? Bring the table. Bring the chairs.

(HARRY *and* LUDDY *start to move the table,* MATT *and*
PERCY *each start to move a chair, with the Servants following with flagons, etc.*)

HENSLOWE: (*Banging the floor with her cane.*) Gentleman!
Gentleman! Be still!

(ALL *freeze and turn towards her. She rises with difficulty.*)

That is Her Majesty's property—and you may not dis-
port it in this fashion. You, sir—put that chair down!

(PERCY, *with chair raised, does not know what to do.*)

Put it down, sir!

(PERCY *deposits the chair and meekly sits on it.*)

NED: (*With mock humility.*) Madam, all we have of comfort is Her Majesty's indulgence—this small table—these tiny chairs and this utterly inadequate food—honey cakes and bits of chicken. May we not partake of this repast?

HENSLOWE: Agh! I have no mind for such things any more. There is too much else. Too much else . . . (*To others.*) Do as you are asked. I will be deputy. (*To* NED.) And you, sir—I will have wine.

(*The others applaud and spring into action. They reprise the last two lines of the song: "Converting all your sounds of woe . . ."*
WILL *finds wine and brings it to* HENSLOWE. *In the meantime,* HENSLOWE*'s chair is moved, and she is reseated while the table, gilt chairs, and accoutrements are set in place. Servants bring the baskets and set out plates and goblets.*)

NED: Now—for our guests.

(*He crosses up to the skips and brings two scarlet tunics, setting them out on the backs of chairs.* JACK *retrieves his tunic from the loft and throws it to* NED.)

LUDDY: (*Meanwhile.*) He's gone mad.

PERCY: I seen a man once, walking naked through the
streets. Mad as they come. Said he'd been driven from
Eden. "Show me the way to go home." Pagh! Them as
knew where Eden was would be as mad as he. He was
caged and carted soon enough.

(MUSIC.
*The* LIGHTS *alter, isolating the table and the chairs.*)

---

## SCENE FOUR

(*Finished with the tunics,* NED *spies* ELIZABETH *about
to enter.*)

NED: Aha! I could have written this myself. Ladies and
gentleman! The Queen!

(ELIZABETH *enters.* HENSLOWE *and female Servants
curtsy, others bow.* ELIZABETH *now wears the black
gown.* STANLEY *follows, carrying* ELIZABETH*'s white
gown, and hands it to* TARDY, *who has followed her.* TOM
*and* BEN *enter.* NED *seats* ELIZABETH *at the table—
after which the others fall back into the shadows.*)

ELIZABETH: Since I have chosen to be *with* you, I have
elected to be *one* of you. And to that end—(*To* NED.) I

am wearing the gown in which your Beatrice mourned the death of Hero.

NED: An interesting choice, Your Grace, given that Hero lived. Are you telling us your hero, too, shall live?

ELIZABETH: Yes. England is my hero. There is no other.

NED: Let us see.

(*He indicates that* WILL *should be seated beside the Queen and pours wine into their goblets.*)

ELIZABETH: I smell mischief, sir.

NED: Mischief is as mischief does, Madam. (*He smiles.*) Behold!

(HENSLOWE *sits, and the others settle into comfortable positions and become an audience.*)

Three captains here . . . (*The tunics.*) They are known to all of us. (*He moves to each tunic as he identifies them.*) Yours, Madam. Yours, sir. And mine.

(*He holds up the notebook.*)

               "Come,
Let's have one other gaudy night: call to me
All my sad captains; fill our bowls once more:

Let's mock the midnight bell."

To the captains!

ELIZABETH: (*Drinking, mystified.*) Come to the purpose.

NED: Three captains, three stories. Love stories. Yes? To be spoken in front of witnesses.

PERCY: "Then must you speak of three that loved not wisely, but too well . . ."

ALL: (*Together.*) Shush!

ELIZABETH: Fool, come and sit near me. I would share your wisdom.

(PERCY *brings a stool and sits.*)

NED: Let us begin with the Master of Words . . . (*To* WILL.) You've had a lot to say about love. As for the thing itself, we know that you have loved—and some of us know it well . . .

(WILL *looks away.* ELIZABETH *takes note of this.*)

But you wear a mask, thinking that no one can read it. Yet this man here . . . (*He lifts the tunic nearest* WILL *and holds it out.*) . . . now Towered and despised, now shunned—was once the centre of all your yearning. Is that not so?

(NED *stands behind* WILL, *draws the tunic around him like a bib, and folds its arms about* WILL's *neck.*)

Is it not so?

(WILL *reaches for the arms and lays the tunic in his lap.*)

WILL: Yes.

NED: I can't hear you.

WILL: *Yes!!* Damn you.

NED: (*Reciting.*)
"A woman's face with Nature's soft hand painted
Hast thou, the master-mistress of . . ."

I can't remember.

(WILL *drapes the tunic on the empty chair's back.*)

WILL: (*Reciting.*)
"A woman's face with Nature's own hand painted
Hast thou, the master-mistress of my passion;
A woman's gentle heart, but not acquainted
With shifting change, as is false women's fashion . . ."

ELIZABETH: (*To* WILL.) Such a scandalous opinion of
women . . .

WILL:

"An eye more bright than theirs, less false in rolling,
Gilding the object whereupon it gazeth;
A man in hue, all hues in his controlling,
Which steals men's eyes and women's souls amazeth.
And for a woman wert thou first created,
Till Nature as she wrought thee fell a-doting,
And by addition me of thee defeated,
By adding one thing to my purpose nothing . . ."

(WILL *pronounces the final word: "no thing."*)

NED: Hah!

WILL:

"But since she prick'd thee out for women's pleasure,
Mine be thy love, and thy love's use their treasure."

(WILL *sits. There is some laughter.*)

ELIZABETH: (*Applauding.*) You have a good wit, sir. And
the grace to turn it on yourself. Well said.

(*The others applaud.*)

Mary—more wine.

(*She gestures to* WILL *and* NED.
WILL *removes the cap.*)

STANLEY: Your Grace.

(*She exits to the courtyard.*)

NED: One thing to *your* purpose nothing? (*Privately, to* WILL.) And pigs have wings—is that it? What—*never?*

WILL: (*Possibly lying.*) Never. Not with him.

(STANLEY *returns with a flagon and a glass for* PERCY *and begins serving wine.*)

NED: You poor sod. All that love, and nothing for it to feed on. So here you sit, and never had your captain.

WILL: There are more ways of *having* than one.

NED: Are there, now. Well, whatever ways you mean, they aren't the ways of love I know.

(WILL *puts the cap on.*)

(*As* STANLEY *pours wine.*) Ah, yes—behold the woman. Busy, busy—oh, so lovely. (*To* WILL.) Can you smell her? I can. All that golden-brown hair. And real, no doubt. (*To* STANLEY.) What's it like to play a woman and be one at the same time? Eh? You could give your mistress lessons.

(STANLEY *slaps him.*)

Ah, no. Too late. She's already given *you* lessons. I could play you—though young Harry there could do it better. The stance is excellent—proud and wary all at once. See that, Harry? The jutting chin—the quivering lip. Don't bite it! No—a brave girl never bites her lip. Harry would never do that. Harry knows better—why don't you? Did Hero bite her lip when she was betrayed? Never.

ELIZABETH: She fainted.

NED: Dead away. Dead. And you, Madam—did you faint when you heard of your lover's betrayal? Ah, no. It would be too *womanly*—and we mustn't have that.

(*The bell rings five times.*
*Pause.*)

ELIZABETH: Five. Surely not five so soon.

STANLEY: Yes, Madam.

ELIZABETH: Two hours left. Only two. Oh, God . . . Where is Pygmy? Where is Cecil? Why has he not returned?

NED: Perhaps he has delayed his return for fear that when he comes he will find a woman in your place. Was that not our bargain?

ELIZABETH: Yes...

NED: (*Holding up the notebook.*) Here, Madam, is a descrip-
tion worthy of your captain. (*Then, sotto voce to* WILL.)
The play's the thing, wherein I'll catch the woman in
the Queen. (*Now, to* ELIZABETH.) I think it would be
fitting if the Queen of England were to read the Queen
of Egypt.

(*The others applaud.*)

ELIZABETH: I warn you—I shall not be ridiculed.

NED: If Madam would but read ...

(*He hands her the book.*)

ELIZABETH: (*Rising and reading.*)
"His legs bestrid the ocean; his reared arm
Crested the world; his voice was propertied
As all the tuned spheres, and that to friends;
But when he meant to quail and shake the orb,
He was as rattling thunder ..." (*She stops.*)

I do not like this. I will say no more. (*She hands the book
to* NED. *To* WILL.) Essex is not a god! You make him
seem like a god! You belittle him with too much praise.

WILL: This is the theatre, Madam, where men play gods
every day.

NED: No, Madam. Do not sit. There is more.

ELIZABETH: I said I would say no more.

NED: But the woman, Majesty. Have we not come here for the woman?

ELIZABETH: I no longer know that I want her.

NED: Because you are afraid of her—afraid she will forgive—and pardon.

ELIZABETH: I say I do not like this.

NED: Like it or not—we still await the woman. (*He has found the page he wants and hands her the book.*) I will be your Antony.

ELIZABETH: And what is the occasion? I must know the occasion.

NED: They are parting, Madam. Antony, in Egypt, has been recalled to Rome. His wife has died. Fulvia.

ELIZABETH: It does not interest me.

NED: It should. Cleopatra knows there is a more important reason for his leave-taking.

ELIZABETH: Yes?

NED: Yes. She suspects . . .

WILL: *Knows* . . .

NED: Antony is in danger of making an alliance with her enemies.

ELIZABETH: Ireland . . .

WILL: Rome.

ELIZABETH: Ireland. This is Essex indeed . . . the very same. It is what he did. Precisely.

(NED *puts on* JACK's *tunic.*)

WILL: As you say, Madam.

ELIZABETH: As I know. Do not slight my awareness.

NED: And so " . . . I will leave you, lady."

(ELIZABETH *does not respond.*)

Majesty? The book . . .

ELIZABETH: Yes.

NED: *I will leave you, lady.*

ELIZABETH: (*Reading.*)
>                   "Courteous lord, one word.
>         Sir, you and I must part, but that's not it;
>         Sir, you and I have loved, but there's not it;
>         That you know well: something it is I would—
>         O, my oblivion is a very Antony,
>         And I am all forgotten."

JACK:
>                   "But that your royalty
>         Holds idleness your subject, I should take you
>         For idleness itself."

ELIZABETH:
>                   " 'Tis sweating labour
>         To bear such idleness so near the heart
>         As Cleopatra this. Your honour calls you hence;
>         Therefore, be deaf to my unpitied folly,
>         And all the gods go with you . . ."

(*She hesitates.*)

No. I will not say this next. I cannot and I will not be a traitor to myself.

NED: Then, there can be no woman. She says: "Upon your sword sit laurel victory!"

ELIZABETH: How can a woman say that to a man she knows is going to betray her?

NED: Antony *fell* upon his sword. I would call that a victory—wouldn't you?

ELIZABETH: My Lord Essex had ample opportunity to do the same—and did not.

NED: Are you not his sword, Madam? Did he not "fall" on you?

WILL: He tripped.

ELIZABETH: You would make light of any death you had not written.

WILL: Death is death, Madam. It comes—we go.

ELIZABETH: Yet I am here.

WILL: In your time, you too will die. But that is not yet. Not yet.

ELIZABETH: In your reading of me, am I to fall upon my sword?

WILL: In my reading, Madam, you already have.

ELIZABETH: Then you misread me altogether. I shall die of regret.

WILL: For what reason?

ELIZABETH: For never having been myself. Which is
more than can be said of Master Lowenscroft, whose
only concern is himself. He urges me to be a woman,
grieving the death of Essex—when the only death he
grieves is his own. (*To* NED.) Where is *your* captain's
death in all of this? I have not yet seen *you* mourn him.

(NED *takes* JACK *to the "playing area."* JACK *lies down
and becomes* NED*'s dead captain.*)

NED:
> "Noblest of men, woulds't die?
> Hast thou no care of me? Shall I abide
> In this dull world, which in thy absence is
> No better than a sty? O see my women,
> The crown of the earth doth melt. My lord!
> O, withered is the garland of war,
> The soldier's pole is fall'n; young boys and girls
> Are level now with men; the odds is gone,
> And there is nothing left remarkable
> Beneath the visiting moon."

(ALL *are deeply moved—including* NED, *who rises and
moves away.*)

I saw him first in the yard of Bell's Inn. Six years ago . . .
I was sitting on the steps—top step leading onto the
porches—drinking ale in the sun. *Clatter—clatter*—I can
hear it still, the sound of his arrival. His horse was
frisky—nervous. When the stable boy came to hold her,

my captain got down and laughed and gave his mare a
slap and I heard his voice . . .

JACK: "I won't be wanting her till morning, lad . . ."

NED: The hair on the back of my neck and all down my
arms stood up. He came across the yard—and his boots
. . . I could hear all the leather on him—smell it. Taste it,
almost. He came and looked at me as if I was a curios-
ity—me staring back like an imbecile.

JACK: "Hello . . ."

NED: Hello. And he passed. When I could move, I found
him in the tap-room—waiting for me.

JACK: "I'm laying over here, tonight. Will you lay over
with me?"

NED: He didn't even ask my name. I knew he was a captain. That I knew. Everything he said, he took for
granted was to be obeyed.

(*He picks up the tunic and smells it.*)

Nothing, nothing, nothing smells like a man. The smell
of his skin, the smell of his hair . . .

(*He puts on the tunic.*)

How was I to know? When I put him on—when I wore
him—how could I know? There wasn't a mark—not a
single mark of disease on any part of him. Only his
wounds and scars—only his soldier-self that had been
to the wars and back. But nothing else. Nothing that
said *beware—take care.* I never knew such loving—
never. Yes. It was rutting. Yes. It was bloody . . .

(ELIZABETH *puts out her hand towards him.* PERCY
*places his hand on hers.*)

Yes. There was hours of it. Hours and hours. All that
night—and all the next week. Hours—minutes—seconds. Seconds—minutes—hours. We made love—we
sang songs—we ate and drank together . . . We told the
stories of our lives . . . We laughed—we wept—we
rejoiced . . . I missed a whole week's performances . . .

PERCY: We all thought you were dead . . .

NED: I was—to everything but life.

(*He removes the tunic and puts it back on the chair.*)

Then he was gone. (*Beat.*) To Ireland. And one of those
endless Irish wars.

ELIZABETH: Ireland. Yes. Where all unhappy stories end
. . . Did he know?

NED: What? That he had poxed me? Maybe. Maybe not. I only knew there was desperation in him. Panic. But no regret. None.

(*Suddenly, he laughs.*)

ELIZABETH: What?

NED: At least I bested my mother. All she got of you was a common sailor. My father. But what I got of you was a captain. And I thank you for him. And for his death. And for my own.

ELIZABETH: *Long live death*—is that it? You are as petulant as Essex in the Tower. You're just another self-centred *boy*. Like him, all you want is someone's everlasting attention.

NED: I'm an actor, Madam.

ELIZABETH: Then play the man!!

NED: I don't know how. It's not my profession.

ELIZABETH: Oh! You are the Prince of Petulance! He could take lessons from you.

NED: May the Prince leave?

ELIZABETH: No. I've not finished. Neither have you. I'm still waiting for the man.

NED: And I am still waiting for the woman.

ELIZABETH: Then you can wait until you rot. She will not be forthcoming. Go. And good riddance.

(NED *begins to exit up right.* HARRY *begins to follow him.*)

NED: Stay back.

HARRY: I only . . .

NED: Stay back!!

(BEAR *cries, off.*)

Or I will kill you!

(HARRY *steps back.* NED *speaks to* ELIZABETH.)

There. Was that man enough for you?

(*He exits.* ELIZABETH *signals to Servants to move the table and chairs upstage.*)

## SCENE FIVE

(WILL *removes the scholar's cap.*)

ELIZABETH: Master Shakespeare?

WILL: Your Grace.

ELIZABETH: *Is* this a play we are in?

WILL: It would seem so, yes.

ELIZABETH: And what will you call it—this play?

WILL: It can have no name until it is finished.

ELIZABETH: And it will not be finished until my Lord Essex is dead? Is that right?

WILL: Perhaps . . .

ELIZABETH: I do not like "perhaps." You enjoy killing?

WILL: Do you?

ELIZABETH: Is Cleopatra's death already written for Master Lowenscroft?

WILL: Yes—but . . .

ELIZABETH: He believes he will not live to play it. I
wrote a death once. Well written—well played. When
Mary Stuart entered the great hall where she would
die, *she* was wearing black. And when the black was
stripped away, she presented herself in crimson to her
executioner. In crimson silks. A great queen—a great
actor. Tell Master Lowenscroft: that is how a great
queen goes to meet death. Not as its subject—but as its
sovereign.

(WILL *puts on the scholar's cap.*)

## SCENE SIX

ELIZABETH: Mistress Tardwell, have you a glass?

TARDY: Oh, yes, Madam. All actors need a glass. There
must be a dozen here.

ELIZABETH: Bring one. And colours. Powder.

(TARDY *goes to the skips and rummages.* WILL *pushes his
cap back on.*)

Mary . . .

STANLEY: Majesty?

ELIZABETH: (*Moving to sit in the prince's chair.*) Come and be my woman. Quickly.

(STANLEY *kneels before* ELIZABETH *and takes her hands.*)

Child—child. Oh, child. You . . . you are so . . .

HENSLOWE: (*Attempting to stand.*) I should like to rise.

ELIZABETH: (*To* PERCY.) Fool—help the Countess to her feet.

(PERCY *hurries to* HENSLOWE *and his attempt to get her standing becomes a little dance.*)

HENSLOWE: Oh, oh, oh . . .

PERCY: Stay. Stay. Stay!

(HENSLOWE *falls back. They try again.*)

HENSLOWE: Oh, oh, oh. Oh! *Oh!*

PERCY: There now—done.

(TARDY *brings a mirror, linen, make-up, and powder to* ELIZABETH. *Servants have already brought a bench to be used as a make-up table.*)

TARDY: Here's what we have, Madam. All we lack is a decent red.

PERCY: (*To* HENSLOWE.) Don't move.

(*He starts towards the loft.*)

TARDY: That Lowenscroft, he used it all in the final act.

PERCY: I have red. (*To* HENSLOWE.) Stay! (*He goes to the loft and retrieves his "Dorothy bag," taking it to* ELIZABETH.) I have here reds to kill. In my lady-days, they would climb up onto the boards and lay their hands on me, as if to drag me down amidst the mob. I used to think: *I will die of wearing red!* But I never gave it up.

HENSLOWE: (*Wavering.*) Oh, oh, oh . . .

(PERCY *hurries to her.*)

I wish to walk.

PERCY: Where, madam?

HENSLOWE: Anywhere but in the yard. I will not go outside. I have not seen the stars in twenty years, and I do not intend to see them now. Give me your arm.

(*She also uses her stick as they commence a walkabout.*)

ELIZABETH: I have been myself for so long. These eyes—
this mouth . . . Mistress Tardwell?

TARDY: Madam?

ELIZABETH: Tell me—*anything*—of real life.

TARDY: Your Majesty lives a real life. One can see that.
May one say this? Your Grace, you claim to lack a
woman. But see here, Madam. (*The mirror.*) There is no
woman lacking here. *I* see you. I see you with every
breath you take. I, too, have lived your life. One man—
another. All are equal in their treachery. *But*—and oh,
Madam, if I could give you this—the joy of *one* child.
Many died—but one lived. And that child will see me
to my death.

ELIZABETH: (*Staring at the mirror.*) Where is Hero?
There's a woman.

(HARRY *steps forward.*)

Look at him, Mary. Your equivalent in every way but
one. (*To* HARRY.) What are you most? In there, where
you live.

HARRY: Myself.

ELIZABETH: You play the woman so well. How can that
be? You're just a boy.

HARRY: I've played the woman all my life.

ELIZABETH: Always the woman? Are you afraid to be a
man?

HARRY: I am a man.

ELIZABETH: (*Handing him the mirror.*) Hold this for me so
that I can see.

HARRY: In April, I will be nineteen—and then I'll be too
old to play in skirts.

ELIZABETH: But, Master Lowenscroft . . .

HARRY: When Ned's a hundred, he'll still be the greatest
player of women.

ELIZABETH: Mary—my hair.

(STANLEY *removes* ELIZABETH*'s wig and sets it aside.
The Queen is bald.*)

So, Master Pearle, you stand amazed. Beneath *your*
woman's hair, you say there is a man. Without my
woman's hair—must I also be a man?

HARRY: No, Majesty.

ELIZABETH: It pleases me that someone will say so. I

cannot bring myself to say it. (*To* TARDY.) More powder, some colour. Hold the glass, boy. (*To* STANLEY.) I should like more wine.

(NED *enters. He wears a long white gown over his shirt and tights. It is neither male nor female. He draws ale and stands watching.* PERCY *reseats* HENSLOWE *in her chair. She holds out her empty glass. A Servant brings wine to them both and to* ELIZABETH.)

Red.

(*She studies her reflection. She reaches into* PERCY's *"Dorothy bag" and finds a pot of red.*)

When I was first a queen, I was twenty-five years old. There is much value in youth . . .

WILL: But more in age.

ELIZABETH: So you say—but where is the proof of it?

WILL: We are here, Madam.

ELIZABETH: There. Done.

(STANLEY *moves to put* ELIZABETH's *wig back on, but is stopped by* NED's *voice.*)

NED: No. Not done. This is nothing more than Your

Majesty playing with colour. Too much white, Madam. Too much red. An actor would know better.

ELIZABETH: (*Rising.*) Would he, now.

NED: To find the woman, Madam, you must hide the man. *Sit.*

(ELIZABETH *sits.* NED *uses the linen gently to wipe away the harshness of what* ELIZABETH *has created. He leaves both white and red, but modifies them.*)

ELIZABETH: Your breath smells of drink.

NED: As does yours. Be still.

HENSLOWE: Master Shakespeare?

WILL: Countess?

HENSLOWE: Who is that young man standing next to Lady Stanley?

WILL: He is an actor, madam. His name is Welles. Matthew Welles. You saw him this afternoon as Claudio.

HENSLOWE: He seems to be uncommonly familiar with the lady.

WILL: Perhaps it will be to her advantage, madam.

HENSLOWE: But—an *actor!* It is scandalous.

WILL: No more scandalous than the Queen's current con-
sort. (*He indicates* NED.) Wouldn't you call his behav-
iour at this moment uncommonly familiar? Yet the
Queen appears to welcome it.

HENSLOWE: Madness. *Actors!* Madness.

(NED *has completed his work. Backing away, he takes the
Beatrice wig and places it on* ELIZABETH'*s head and holds
the mirror for her.*)

NED: There, Madam. The complete woman. Such as can be
found.

ELIZABETH: But this is Beatrice.

NED: You wanted a woman—I gave you one.

ELIZABETH: One of yours.

NED: No, Madam. One of many.

ELIZABETH: Oh, yes. You have them all at your fingertips.

NED: As you have many men, Madam, at yours.

(ELIZABETH *strikes* NED. *Pause. He goes to his tankard and drinks, his back to* ELIZABETH.)

---

## SCENE SEVEN

ELIZABETH: Can nothing provoke you, sir?

NED: Provoke me?

ELIZABETH: A man would strike back.

NED: Would he, now?

ELIZABETH: *Yes!*

NED: To what end?

ELIZABETH: To avenge himself.

NED: Of what? A mere lack of courtesy?

ELIZABETH: I struck you, sir. Reply.

NED: Ah, so. I see. In your woman's guise, you still act the man—and expect me to do likewise. But that's too easy. You want a man? I'll give you a man.

(*He goes to the skip and rummages. He withdraws an object which he hides behind him. He also draws an*

*unsheathed sword from the skip. With them, he advances
on* ELIZABETH.
*The others shout. The* BEAR *calls, off.*)

STANLEY: Stop!

HARRY, JACK, and MATT: (*Together.*) Ned! Ned! For
    God's sake!

(NED *raises the sword.* STANLEY *screams.* NED *brings
the blade crashing to the floor, and raises the hidden object
above him. It is a severed "head' with long dark hair and a
gory neck.*)

NED: Here, Majesty, is the only man you need! *God save the
    Queen!!*

ELIZABETH: Oh, dear Jesus Christ.

(*She falls to her knees. The others are still.* NED *lowers the
"head" and looks into its face.*)

NED: "O, see my women . . . the crown of the earth doth
    melt." (*He kisses the lips.*) "My lord . . ."

(*Hanging the head from a lantern pole,* NED *crosses down-
stage, dropping the sword as he passes* ELIZABETH, *who
sags and sits on her hip.*)

ELIZABETH: Get me up.

NED: Get yourself up.

ELIZABETH: *Get me up!!*

(*Everyone freezes.* ELIZABETH *reaches for the sword and uses it to push herself up. She advances on* NED —*raises the sword and brings it down by his side.* NED *does not move.*)

NED: Next thing we know, Your Majesty will seek employment at the Tower. What is your headsman's name, Madam?

ELIZABETH: What sort of idiot question is that?

NED: What's his name? *History* will want to record it—lest the people think his name was *Elizabeth.*

ELIZABETH: Pah!

NED: Poor old headsman. Nobody knows his name. Left entirely out of history—not a single mention. I think he deserves a name. Don't you? Think of it—in the morning—when?—at seven? Two apparently *nameless men* will meet in the courtyard of the Tower. The one whose name you refuse to voice—and the anonymous headsman. What on earth can history do with that?

ELIZABETH: It can tell the truth.

NED: Which is?

ELIZABETH: That one of them has a name—which you know perfectly well.

NED: Well, no—as a matter of fact, I don't. It's slipped my mind.

ELIZABETH: Essex.

NED: Is that all? Just Essex? Isn't that one of your counties? County Norfolk—County Sussex—County Essex . . .

ELIZABETH: Stop it!

NED: What's his *name?*

ELIZABETH: Devereux.

NED: Devereux. A city in France?

ELIZABETH: Stop it!!

NED: Not until I have his name.

ELIZABETH: Robert.

NED: And between the sheets?

ELIZABETH: Oh, God. Make him stop.

NED: There was a time between the sheets—yes? And

whatever happened there—whatever it was—whether
everything or nothing—there was a time when he was
there with you and you were there with him. And if
you cannot mourn that moment, two nameless men
*will* meet in the morning and both will be forgotten forever. Madam?

ELIZABETH: Robin.

(*She goes to get a drink, and stands with her back to the
others.*)

NED: I thought I heard a woman there just then. Or something of a woman. That catch in the throat that comes
only when speaking a lover's name—Troilus—
Romeo—Antony—Robin . . .

ELIZABETH: Captain!

NED: Yes—and "Captain."

(*The dogs bark.*)

ELIZABETH: There is too much woman in you, sir—it
seems to me.

NED: Are you daring me to bed you?

HENSLOWE: Master Lowenscroft!

ELIZABETH: Leave him be!

(*She thrusts her glass at* STANLEY.)

More!

(STANLEY *fills the glass.*)

Now *you* tell me: *what was his name?*

NED: I don't know.

ELIZABETH: Ah, yes. *It's slipped your mind.* Is that it?

NED: Captain.

ELIZABETH: Is that all? Just *Captain.* Surely between the
sheets there must have been more than that. What?

(NED *turns away.*)

Perhaps he was another Robin—or another Harry. Did
you not ask his name?

NED: Yes. Yes—I did.

ELIZABETH: And . . . ?

NED: He said . . . he said his name was . . . Hal.

ELIZABETH: What? I didn't hear you.

NED: Hal.

ELIZABETH: My, my. Another Harry, after all.

NED: He did not say Harry.

ELIZABETH: No. He said . . . (*She whispers.*) *Hal.* Do you mourn him?

NED: Yes.

ELIZABETH: As a man—or as a woman?

NED: As a man.

ELIZABETH: And yet, you weep.

NED: Men do that, Madam—from time to time.

---

## SCENE EIGHT

ELIZABETH: Tell me the hour. Someone—seek the watch. He will know. (*To* LUDDY.) You.

(LUDDY *goes into the yard. Dogs bark.*)

Where is Cecil? What delays him? *Why does he not come?!* Oh, damn the dogs! *Damn them!!*

(STANLEY *hurries out. The dogs quieten.* ELIZABETH *sits.*)

We are all in the Tower. Towered. All of us. In this hateful moment.

WILL: If we *were* in the Tower, Madam, lives might be saved.

ELIZABETH: You damn me unfairly. You have the advantage of being unable to pardon. Only I and I alone can pardon. It is a weight you do not bear.

(LUDDY *and* STANLEY *return.*)

LUDDY: A quarter from the hour, Madam.

ELIZABETH: Which hour?

LUDDY: Six, Your Majesty.

ELIZABETH: Six. *Oh, where is Cecil!!*

(*She sees* LUDDY *begin to walk away.*)

You, sir.

LUDDY: Madam?

ELIZABETH: You remind me of my father.

LUDDY: It is true I have his beard.

ELIZABETH: Also his girth, though he stood better.

(LUDDY *laughs nervously and "performs" Henry VIII.*)

Whenever I think of the Tower, I think of my father.
His breath, like yours, was fouled with food and drink.
His hands, like yours, were fat and filthy. He fore-
swore gloves as being *effeminate.* Besides, his fingers
must be free, with so many laces to untie. All women
were his—my father's. He was the King. Manhood
was his profession.

NED: And yours.

ELIZABETH: No, sir. My name is not Harry. The only
skirts I hoist are my own. (*To* WILL.) There was no
England in him—only him*self.* Only Harry—only ever
Harry. My father. *God*, if I could kill every man in my
kingdom, I would do it in a second!! There is *not one*
worthy of this moment.

STANLEY: Madam—be at peace.

ELIZABETH: Peace? The world is ending. Even I cannot
prevent it. (*To* NED.) Neither can you. You cannot
avoid your death any more than Essex can in the

Tower. Do what you will, it will come.

NED: No. Not yet.

ELIZABETH: Not yet. *Not yet.* I predict these will be your last words. And will you also say: *I will not go*? Perhaps you could ask Master Shakespeare to write it for you. Another Juliet. Dead—but not dead. (*Beat.*) How will it be? And where?

NED: In a ditch, somewhere.

ELIZABETH: In a ditch? You have no more sense of honour than to find yourself a ditch?

NED: What have I to do with honour?

ELIZABETH: Everything. Look at you, standing there! The greatest actor of women in our time. You have the talent and the body of a god. Pay them your respect. Give them a decent farewell.

NED: I barely know who they are. There's been so little time.

ELIZABETH: But enough to take some joy from them.

NED: Joy, Madam?

ELIZABETH: Joy in your captain! Joy in your Beatrice! Joy

in your comradeship with all these others! To have
been so alive! Master Lowenscroft, here we are learning
how to go on living—by learning how to die. But to
die—even at your age—is not to have failed to have a
life. (*She turns to the others.*) Yes?

(*The others applaud.*
*The* BEAR *enters and "speaks." He has wakened and is look-*
*ing for* NED.)

It seems your friend has arrived to tell you the same
thing.

(NED *turns. The* BEAR *sees him and lopes past the others,*
*standing when he comes to* NED *and holding out his arms.*
*He cries with relief—as though he speaks* NED*'s name.* NED
*embraces him.*)

Will you take him with you to your ditch, Master
Lowenscroft? Or will you send him back to the pit? Not
much difference, is there?

HARRY: There will be no ditch, Madam. And no return to
the pit.

ELIZABETH: You redeem the name of Harry, Master
Pearle. I only hope he heard you.

## SCENE NINE

(*There is a commotion in the yard. Voices and dogs.*)

CECIL: (*Off.*) Get down! Get *down!* Call them off, you idiot!
    *Call them off!!*

(*Shouts and whistling quieten the dogs.* NED *takes the*
BEAR *aside. The* LIGHTS *alter.* CECIL *enters from the*
*courtyard.*)

   Madam . . . Majesty.

ELIZABETH: (*Not turning.*) Is it done?

CECIL: Those dogs!

ELIZABETH: Forget the dogs. The *message.* Is it delivered?

CECIL: Yes.

(CECIL *removes his hat and cloak and hands them to*
TARDY, *who takes them to one of the skips.*)

ELIZABETH: Did you . . . ? Was he present?

CECIL: Yes, Madam.

ELIZABETH: Did he speak?

CECIL: (*Going to the brazier.*) At length, Your Grace.

ELIZABETH: And?

CECIL: He requested of the Lord Lieutenant—that's Sir Walter Badger, Your Grace, a fine reliable fellow . . .

ELIZABETH: I know his name! Come to the words.

CECIL: Madam, I am out of breath.

ELIZABETH: *His words.*

CECIL: His words. Yes. He requested to see the communication of Your Majesty's decision with his own eyes.

ELIZABETH: And . . . ?

CECIL: And it was handed to him.

ELIZABETH: Pygmy!

CECIL: He read it—word for word—twice over.

ELIZABETH: Yes?

CECIL: And when, the second time, he came to Your Majesty's signature . . .

ELIZABETH: What?

CECIL: He kissed it, Madam. Held it for an instant to his breast—and kissed it once again.

ELIZABETH: But what did he say? What did he say?

CECIL: He said, Your Grace, that he craved Your Majesty's forgiveness.

ELIZABETH: Forgiveness. But not my pardon?

CECIL: Madam, your letter expressly stated there would be no pardon.

*(The bell tolls the hour of six. Silence.)*

ELIZABETH: And . . . ?

CECIL: And . . . he submitted to Your Majesty's will.

ELIZABETH: Without a word of protest?

CECIL: None.

ELIZABETH: Was he—is he . . . afraid?

CECIL: Yes.

ELIZABETH: Was it said? Did he say so—*I am afraid.*

CECIL: It was put to him by a priest that, being mortal, his lordship might be fearful, and—"Yes," he said. "Yes, I am. More than once, in battle," he said, "I have been seized by fears I had not imagined possible. But this is worse, because tomorrow is a certainty and if the strength of God is not with me in the morning, I will not know how to stand."

ELIZABETH: He said this?

CECIL: "I am young," he said . . . (*Relishing the words.*) " . . . and I have spent my youth in wantonness, lust, and filth. I have been puffed up with pride and vanity. My sins are more in number than the hairs on my head," he said. And at this point, Madam, he fell to his knees.

ELIZABETH: And . . . the Queen. Did he speak of the Queen?

CECIL: In this way only. Still on his knees, he said to me: "Here before you, I pray for the welfare of Her Majesty the Queen, whose death I protest I never meant. Nor any violence to her person." Then he said: "Say so, Robert. Tell her I said so." And I have done as I was charged.

ELIZABETH: Did he not mention his offence? Nothing of his treason?

CECIL: Nothing of his treason. Only his sins. And his fear.

(*Silence.*)

ELIZABETH: I want to see him.

CECIL: Your Majesty knows that cannot happen.

ELIZABETH: I want to see him.

CECIL: It cannot be allowed. These events must not be reversed. England and Your Majesty would suffer if they were.

ELIZABETH: You think *this* is not suffering? I want to see him!!

CECIL: Madam, you may not. (*To* WILL.) *And she will not!*

(WILL *shrugs. He wants her to go for Southampton's sake.*)

ELIZABETH: Someone . . . someone take me to him. Someone bring him to me. Someone—do something!!

HENSLOWE: Madam—Your Grace—I beg you not to go. For your own sake. The dead are dead.

ELIZABETH: But I must. I must go. I must.

CECIL: Madam—no.

ELIZABETH: Then, send out the horses. Send out the messengers . . .

HENSLOWE: The horses will fall.

ELIZABETH: *One* could arrive.

CECIL: The roads are foul, Madam. Mud—snow—ice. There is no time to reach the destination you require of horses. It is impossible.

ELIZABETH: *No!!*

CECIL: Yes.

ELIZABETH: Oh, God. So . . . here we are—in the moment. (*She sits.*) You, sir—Master Edmund . . .

(JACK *goes to her. She stares at him.*)

You were once, to me, so beautiful . . . (*She touches his face.*) And once, you were all my life.

JACK: Madam, yet again you mistake me.

ELIZABETH: Hush. Be still. I know who you are—another Irish upstart—with opinions counter to my own. And yet, you embody his beauty—and for that reason, you are forgiven.

(JACK *retreats.*)

*Elizabeth Rex. (To* WILL.) There's your title, sir. *Elizabeth Rex, the Queen.* Have me say that "all my life, for the sake of my kingdom, I have played the Prince." And have me say that, "for the sake of my kingdom, I willingly took up the sword of the headsman and brought it down where I would rather kiss." And have me say . . . Have me say . . .

STANLEY: Madam . . .

ELIZABETH: I cannot achieve this moment. How does one say *goodbye?*

NED: I can show you.

ELIZABETH: You would go to the Tower in my place?

NED: I would go in your person.

CECIL: Never. This must not happen.

WILL: It strikes me, Your Majesty, my Lord Cecil is too anxious to keep you from the Tower. He fears the woman in you might undo his present and his future powers.

CECIL: Prattle.

WILL: Is it?

CECIL: I will not argue this. She will not go. And none shall go in her place.

NED: Person. (*He smiles.*) There's a difference.

(*The* LIGHTS *alter.*
*There is* MUSIC *and the* SOUND *of water. A falcon cries overhead. Voices.*)

(*Echo effect.*) Robin?

(JACK *steps forward into a pool of* LIGHT.)

JACK: (*Echo effect.*) Madam?

(*The echo effect fades over the next few speeches.*)

NED: No, not Madam. Not Majesty. Don't you remember?

JACK: What, Madam?

NED: My name. My *name.*

JACK: Elizabeth . . .

(*Falcon cry.*)

NED: Not *Elizabeth. Bess.*

(NED *moves into the* LIGHT. *They face each other.*)

You were my Robin—I was your Bess. I have come to die with you.

(JACK *falls to his knees.* NED *caresses his head.*)

We will die together. Which is fitting. In killing you—I kill myself. How did we come to this moment?

JACK: Love.

NED: No. Ambition. You to be you—and me to be me.

(ELIZABETH *moves into the* LIGHT. JACK *embraces* NED's *waist.*)

JACK: I love you.

NED: Yes. And I you. Nothing will remain of me when you are gone. I renege my right to the man who killed you. He is dead—and only I am left.

ELIZABETH: (*She reaches out.*) Robin?

(*Falcon cry.*
*The* LIGHT *fades on* NED *and* JACK, *and rises on* WILL.)

WILL: Would you go there? To be with him?

ELIZABETH: No. He is gone.

WILL: Madam, you, too, can conjure him.

ELIZABETH: I don't know how.

WILL: Yes, you do.

(*Falcon cry.*
ELIZABETH *looks up, shading her eyes.*)

You called him once your *hawk*. He sat on your arm.

ELIZABETH: Yes.

WILL: Call him.

ELIZABETH: Where is he?

(*The* LIGHT *rises on* NED. *He has shed his white robe and wears tights and shirt.*)

NED: Here, Bess. With you.

(ELIZABETH *falls to her knees.*)

Are you afraid?

ELIZABETH: Yes. Yes. More than once, I have been seized
by fears I had not imagined possible—in the dark—in the

night—but tomorrow is a certainty—and if your love is not with me in the morning, I will not know how to rise.

NED: You will rise. And I will rise with you. Stand.

ELIZABETH: I will not ask pardon. And there will be none. I have already said so. In this moment it is you who must die. But inside this moment, you will always be present. You were here—and you left your mark. Indelible. On me—and on the time.

NED: Am I to be proud of this?

ELIZABETH: No, Robin. You are to glory in it. *I* did not come here—I could not—but in my heart, I came.

(ELIZABETH *leaves the* LIGHT *and retreats.* NED *is left alone in the pool of* LIGHT.
*Falcon cry.*)

NED: (*Looking up.*) Hal . . . ? Harry . . . ? Hal . . . ? How does one do this? I've done it a hundred times on stage. But you . . . you had to suffer it. And did. On that day, you rose from your bed thinking there was still *forever*. Yet in the afternoon—in the evening—in the twilight—you sank into the earth. Out of all sight forever. How does one do this? How? To be alive—no more. No more the smell of horses or the kiss of leather. No more connections, no more responses. (*He looks at* WILL.) No more wonder. No more words. (*He looks at* HARRY.) No more the warmth of breath—or the touch of fingertips on skin. Of all these joys—no more. All the way over. You're gone. You're safe. Safe. (*He goes to* ELIZABETH.) Madam, here is your man. If I can let him go—I can go myself.

(*The bell begins to toll seven. Everyone is frozen and silent. There is distant cannon fire. The dogs begin to bark. The cannon in the yard is fired. There is a frenzy of barking.* ELIZABETH *gives a cry. Everyone remains still and silent.*)

---

## SCENE TEN

(*The* LIGHTS *alter.*)

CECIL: Madam, the hour for matins has arrived.

ELIZABETH: Has it? So, you would go to pray?

CECIL: I pray every day, Majesty.

ELIZABETH: Do you? I would not have guessed it.

CECIL: Yes—I do. Every day.

ELIZABETH: Why? You need not fear, Robert. You will survive me. You are too clever not to.

(CECIL *bows and exits.* ELIZABETH *addresses everyone.*)

The curfew is lifted—I will leave you now. I thank you for your company. I played here as a child—and I have played this night—in this sweet, good place—my final days. (*To* MATT.) Sir, I am not blind. (*Taking* STANLEY*'s hand.*) You, my dear one, all that I might have been, may you have all I might have had. I bless you.

(*She kisses* STANLEY*'s brow and joins her hand in* MATT*'s.* ELIZABETH *turns to* TARDY.)

You, mistress, this (*A ring.*) . . . is for you. And I pray, as it was for me, a token of some fidelity. I had it from my Lord Burleigh. Until his final breath, he was my protector. (*To* WILL.) For you, sir, my words. Use them as you will. I cannot offer you more. Though one thing else would be welcome. Your lord in the Tower shall keep his head. But while I live, he will lose his freedom. (*To* JACK.) For you—a sample of your hatred.

(*She goes to* STANLEY *and removes a locket in which there is a miniature portrait of herself.*)

(*To* STANLEY.) In ridding you of this, I rid you of your vows.

STANLEY: But, Madam—that is your portrait. I . . .

ELIZABETH: You will not miss it. You have me in your heart. (*She goes to* JACK.) This, sir, is all you need to avenge your loss of Ireland. An object on which you may relieve yourself as you will—to no avail. Ireland is mine. (*Then, to* PERCY.) Come with me. Here . . .

PERCY: Madam.

ELIZABETH: "Oh, Fool—I shall go mad . . ." (*She kisses him. Then she turns to* NED.) Master Lowenscroft—I would rather I had known you than anyone, but one, I ever met. I will not forget you. (*To* HARRY.) Nor you, sir. Nor the bear.

(*She caresses the* BEAR's *face and gives him a honey cake. Then she removes her rope of pearls and places them around the* BEAR's *neck.*)

These, I trust, will keep you both from your ditch.

(*She looks all around.*)

Come, Countess—let us go together.

(LUDDY *steps forward expectantly.*)

LUDDY: "God save Your Grace."

(ELIZABETH *ignores him.* LUDDY *falls to his knees, dev-astated.* ELIZABETH *and* HENSLOWE *exit. The others follow—*NED, HARRY, *and the* BEAR.)

WILL: (*Turning to the audience.*) And so, it was done. We had our man—we had our woman—and this way, they passed into time.

(CECIL *returns.*)

CECIL: Master Shakespeare—a word. This story must remain within these walls—for our mutual benefit in the time to come.

(*He exits.*
*A passing-bell is heard.*
WILL *blows out a lantern and takes another in hand. He pockets his notebook and removes the scholar's cap, kisses it, and places it on top of the severed head.*)

WILL: Young Will Shakespeare died this day. Fifty-two years old. Died in his bed. A man of talent, who had an uneventful life. Or so it will be said.

(*We hear the* SOUND *of water, birds, and insects.*)

BOYS: (*Calling from the past.*) Will! Will! Over here—over here!

(WILL *makes a slow exit into the yard.*
*The bell continues to toll.*
*The* LIGHTS *fade until only the sky is lit. Then, blackout.*
*The play ends.*)